STiNKFooT
AN ENGLISH COMIC OPERA

Crackpot Theatre Company
is proud to present its first production

AN ENGLISH COMIC OPERA

Written by
Vivian Stanshall
& Ki Longfellow-Stanshall

Lyrics, Music & Arrangement by
Vivian Stanshall

Directed by
Vivian Stanshall

Produced by
Ki Longfellow-Stanshall
for the Old Profanity Showboat

Introduced by
Ki Longfellow-Stanshall

Published by Sea Urchin Editions

Sea Urchin Editions
PO Box 25212
3001 HE Rotterdam
The Netherlands
www.sea-urchin.net

Hello, dear reader! If you are reading this I can only think it's because somehow, in some way, you - like me - love one of England's greatest national treasures, Vivian Anthony Stanshall. If so, it's my fond belief that you are in for a treat.

You hold in your hands *Stinkfoot*, a thoroughly original musical comedy - or, as Vivian would have it, an English Comic Opera in the Grand Tradition - written by him and written by me for my stage on a thoroughly magical ship called the Thekla. True, it is only the script and a script isn't exactly the 'thing', is it? Where is the music? Where are the lights, the sequins, the shouting? Where the soft silken hiss of an alley cat's menacing meow?

You will have to imagine all that. But then... what else is your imagination for - other than to imagine all the world and everything in it? To imagine even your very self? And then to believe in that you and that world so completely it's sure to kill you in the end. As Vivian said: 'Imagination is all I've ever called Home.'

This little book is a blueprint, a pirate's map of words that could, if all goes well, lead you through a small door into Vivian's large, extraordinary, and labyrinthine mind. It's an invitation to spend a little time in the private rooms of a unique and complex artist.

Stinkfoot is about art. It's about artists. It's about what artists do and who they are and why they can't help themselves. It's about the desperate misery of creation and the self-abandoned joy of it. It's about me. But most of all, it's about Vivian.

What was Vivian like?

He was a loveable buffoon and an irritating madman. He was tender and self-doubting and self-defeating and self-glorifying and wholly self-made. He was all the things you think he was... an honest to god genius whose life was torment and hilarity. He was larger than life and he took up a lot of room. He was wonderful to have around and horrid to have around... it all depends on what day - what hour - we're talking about. I adored him.

Sir Henry would give a great honking snort at what I am about to say next, but Hubert Rawlinson would giggle with joy. After death, the first thing Vivian said to me was: 'Having a wonderful time. Wish you were here.'

What is he doing now? I imagine that Vivian is now enormous and writing a symphony with loud paint.

Why did we write *Stinkfoot*?

Once upon a time, I owned a ship, a real ship - Thekla, the Baltic Trader. I found her laid up in the far north of England in the city of Sunderland, rusted and listing and haunted. She was one hundred and eighty feet long and more than half of that was a huge empty hold. When Vivian and I first set foot in her, two cold sailors huddled together for more than warmth and with the thin Geordie sun shining through an open hatch thirty feet above our heads, we saw her as a salty cathedral. For us, it was no leap at all from cathedral to theater.

The Thekla became The Old Profanity Showboat, chugging her way - without ballast, insurance, or registration, but not without enthusiasm and certainly not without being filmed by the BBC - from Sunderland on the North Sea to Bristol on the Severn, there to open her doors in May of 1983. Twenty seven months later, after I'd worked nonstop to stage, support, coddle, and clean up after at least two hundred outside productions, after bands of every stripe from jazz to punk gunk to moments of sheer terror, after cabaret and art shows and lawsuits and poetry readings (Mark Twain knew what he was talking about when he said: 'Poets who read their work in public may have other bad habits.'), after snits and fits and ART with a capital F, after hip hops and weddings and a truly memorable Hells Angels Weenie Roast, it was time for my people, the people behind the scenes who worked it all, to get on the damn stage. And it was time for Vivian and I to put on a show.

In the beginning, we talked about staging something like *Damn Yankees* since that was a favorite of my 'girls' - the amazing young women who came to the ship as customers, or singers, or actresses, and remained as underpaid, overworked, bar- and scullery-maids. (You will find their names in the cast- or thank you-lists... and proud I am to see them there.) But with Vivian around, the idea that we would do anything other than something totally original, was quickly tossed overboard.

From one minute to another, *Stinkfoot* was born.

Vivian and I wrote the thing in bed. (Although on a ship, I suppose it was more properly a sizable bunk.) Night after night, after whatever had appeared on my stage that evening had taken its last bow and we'd thrown out the last drunk, Vivian and I cuddled beneath the covers in the captain's cabin with pencils and paper and tape recorders and his ukulele, and thrashed out the story and the characters and the meaning - sort of. Actually, the meaning was allowed to fend for itself. I think it took two weeks. Maybe less. We hadn't the luxury of time... for all sorts of good and reasonable reasons, I'd decided it had to go on at Christmas, which is England's Pantomime Season. When we first took to our bunk, it was in the first few days of September, 1985. Silky was six years old. Vivian and I weren't much older. We had a little over three months to write, score, cast, and rehearse both actors and musicians for a full length musical, to design costumes and sets, even hairdos, and to get them made or built or dyed or whatever else was needed, to find props, create programs & posters, do lighting, choreograph I can't remember how many dance numbers, to - oh, my god, were we mad?

It was Vivian's idea to base the musical on *Stinkfoot*, the saucy tale of a New York City alley cat I'd written long before I met Mr. Standstill, something he fell in love with and read as a bedtime story to his son, Rupert, and later to our daughter Silky. Our version was custom made for my faithful, hard-working, crew who had enjoyed or endured two years of other people on Thekla's stage, and for the pick of the local talent who'd made our stage their home. Hence some of its more peculiar peculiarities. If someone could sing, but not act? If someone could act, but not sing? If someone could do neither? If someone could be taught to learn the ukulele? Or could dance but only in one direction? If they played the accordion, walked on their hands, were good with their toes? Somehow, in some way, we made it all fit.

So why did we really write it? Because Vivian and I needed to use the stage just for us. We needed to make something we wanted to see up there - and what better thing than an entire two and a half hour comic opera? Never intending that Thekla would survive the thing financially, with no backers and therefore no restrictions, 'corporate input', or 'interested parties', we could make it without compromise. We could write whatever we wanted, however we wanted. It was my ship. It was our show. It was Vivian's music. We were beholden to no one. It was intoxicating. It was also a hell of a lot of hard bloody work.

What's it about?

Ah. Perhaps if I just inhale and write in a rush on the exhale?

If by 'about' you mean, what's the story? - then the story's about Soliquisto, a once great music hall artiste (based on Vivian as the performer he was in his Bonzo Dog days) whose greatest creation, an

All-Talking, All-Singing, All-Dancing cat, disappeared one night nine years before to his eternally lamented regret. Ever since, Soliquisto's once top-of-the-bill act has gone from the heights of the Albert Hall to an end of a career End-of-The-Pier theater... and the sorrowful Solly believes it's all because he'd lost his greatest work of art. All he has left is his nephew, Buster, and his nephew Buster is... he is - well, he is not Stinkfoot. But he is still young and he's still ambitious and Buster wants more than endless one-night stands for all their slog and sweat. If only the old boy would pass along his 'secret', that hidden something that made his Uncle Soliquisto special, perhaps even a genius, why then, why then - maybe even the Palladium!

Our story begins when Soliquisto and Buster find themselves once again playing the very seaside venue where Solly first discovered Stinkfoot. It's also where Stinkfoot had last been seen, presumed accidentally drowned in the angry sea under this very dressing room. Here too, another of Soliquisto's creations most certainly died. The fate of his songbird, Prince Pollyanna, is no mystery - save for who could have been so cruel as to kill her.

Here, Solly and his Not-So-Dumb-Friends are booked to play for a week. Besides the Great Soliquisto himself, this means Persian Moll, Stinkfoot's once partner (also an all-singing, all-dancing, all-hissing cat - and meee-ow! all female) who is all that's left of Soliquisto's real artistry. It means Buster, who is, amongst other ignoble things, often a stand-in for the incomparable, irreplaceable Stinkfoot. And it most definitely means Screwy, Soliquisto's dummy. It is Screwy who mouths Soliquisto's unceasing menace of self - for no one is crueler to us than ourselves.

But just below the theater on the pier, there is another world. Down underneath, on the rubbishy hard-pebbled shore of England's cold and oily sea, lives Mrs Bag Bag, a fishy Lady of the Bags who finds and treasures things, little things. This is also the home of Isaiah the Flounder (one eye's 'igher than the other), who, buried in sand and in deepest gloom, pines for Polly, Mrs Bag Bag's foundling budgerigar. Here too swims Elma, the Electrified Eel, who lives only to dive.

It's down here with Mrs B. that Stinkfoot and Moll were kittens together. And here where an egg from Prince Pollyanna's cage fell the night she was killed.

Under the pier, it's a world of the lost and disregarded: partly cooked shrimps and woeful sirens and drowned sailors and horrid cocklers and giant squid.

It's to this Under-The-Pier world that Stinkfoot comes home again.

Does this make sense? Does it have to? Does one really have to talk about the lands of under and over, of diving deep and keeping in bags? Of animals who sing and dummies who dance and a bag lady who knows the future even if it never happens and an old man made young again by following his nose? Need we dissect Vivian's seaside boyhood at the mouth of the Thames? Or the English Music Hall that touched him so? Or even look for bits of me (a California Yankee at Rawlinson End) in all this?

Stinkfoot makes sense to me. It made sense to Vivian - or as much sense as he was capable of. Vivian was not a sensible man. *Stinkfoot* is not a sensible show. It's music hall. It's Broadway. It's dada. It's surreal and it's magical and it talks about art. Art is what comes off an artist as steam comes off a kettle. Art is a well - no matter how often you dip in your cup, is it ever empty? If Stinkfoot has a lesson, it's this: make what you must make, and let the creatures of your artful heart go. Once made, they are what they are... they will live with you or without you. Or they will die. That is, if anything ever dies. But you, you are an artist, and an artist can always make more. And more. (When someone once asked Vivian if he minded other artists stealing from him, and almost always without credit, Vivian answered, 'Not as much as I might, amigo, for I can always make more.')

If *Stinkfoot* has a moral, perhaps it's this: Follow Your Nose.

Stinkfoot was staged twice. The best-by-far and most glorious production was the first production. It was directed by Vivian and staged by me. It was written for my ship, and for her one-of-a-kind stage.

For over two weeks, people came to see Thekla's *Stinkfoot* from all over Britain. People came from continental Europe. People came from the United States. Night after night people came, and when there were no seats left, they brought their own cushions, and huddled on the jarrah wood decking until there was no floor space left... for without a doubt the ship and *Stinkfoot* were dearly loved - and still are by all who sailed in them.

I have a video of a single performance of our comic opera, perhaps the second night, perhaps the third. It is badly lit because we would not allow the cameraman to ruin the 'theater of it' by using his lights, badly recorded because he was required to stay well away from the stage, but even so, even so - on it Stinkfoot lives. And just towards the end, well into the final scene of the Second Act, suddenly... Vivian's laughter rings out as plain as plain. Somewhere in the dark, Vivian was watching that night, and his great round laugh, full of a boy's pure delight, is captured there. Somehow, I'm sure he knew I would listen one day, so many years later, and that by this laugh, always remember what Stinkfoot meant to him, and to me.

Perhaps you too - someone out there in the dark and holding this little book in your hands - will find our Comic Opera in the Grand Tradition means something to you as well. If I wish nothing else for you, I wish you could hear Vivian laugh.

Ki Longfellow-Stanshall, March 5, 2002

Seven years, Vivian... it's been seven years.

AN ENGLISH COMIC OPERA

by
Vivian Stanshall
& Ki Longfellow-Stanshall

All lyrics* & music written by
Vivian Stanshall

originally produced by
Ki Longfellow-Stanshall
for the Old Profanity Showboat, Bristol, England

* except IMAGINATION, IT'S MURDER LIVING NEXT DOOR
& DROWNED SAILOR'S DREAM written by Stanshall & Longfellow-Stanshall

Characters
(in order of appearance)

BUSTER
SCREWY
STINKFOOT
PRINCE POLLYANNA, THE QUEEN OF SONGBIRDS
PERSIAN MOLL
THE COASTGUARD
THREE WOEFUL SIRENS
THE GREAT SOLIQUISTO
ISAIAH, THE FLOUNDER
POLLY, THE FOUNDLING BUDGERIGAR
ELMA, THE ELECTRIFYING ELVER
THE BALANCED NOSE
MRS BAG BAG
GOD
THE DROWNED SAILOR
THE PARTLY COOKED SHRIMP
THE HORRID COCKLER
THE GIANT SQUID
THE PUBLIC
THE LEFT SIDE OF SCREWY'S BRAIN
THE RIGHT SIDE OF SCREWY'S BRAIN

ACT ONE,
SCENE ONE.

Darkened stage, comes whistling wind & the scraping of a key in a lock.

Lights half-up on a backstage dressing room in an End-Of-The-Pier Pavilion. A door opens: creeeak! Outlined in its light, the figure of a man, caped and top-hatted. Closing the door, he snaps on a torch. Its beam, quick & furtive, seeks out & finds, 1st: a big poster of Prince Pollyanna, the Queen of Song Birds, 2nd: a much bigger poster announcing the 5-Night Top-of-the-Bill Appearance of the World Famous Great Soliquisto & His Not-So-Dumb Friends (ably assisted by the talented Buster), 3rd: a large travelling trunk, and 4th: a shiny, overlarge, saw.

Buster (for this is Soliquisto's nephew & 'faithful' assistant) sets his torch where it will light only the trunk, then seizes the saw. Lifting the lid of the trunk, he tugs out Screwy, a wooden dummy, by the scruff of its huge collar.

Holding the dummy steady, Buster's face is a picture of fevered lunacy.

BUSTER *(dark & breathy)* - I must have the secret! And the secret is in this dummy! All in the mind, is it? Then we must have it out!

Dramatically lit, Buster saws vigorously down Screwy's ghastly forehead. (Screechful sound of ripping hardwood.)

Suddenly, the air is rent with the awksome squawk of a distressed parrot. Dropping Screwy (but not the saw), Buster grabs his torch, waving it wildly over audience and dressing room. The moment the light finds the door, Stinkfoot enters with a Cagney bound, trumpet in hand.

STINKFOOT - 'Allo, Buster! Say? What's with the DIY? And why, might I arsk, at this time o'night?

Aghast, Buster tries stuffing Screwy back in the trunk. Struggling with saw & dummy & torch, he spotlights Stinkfoot, who reacts with loads of hammy pizzazz.

STINKFOOT - Curtain up! Light the light! *(plays a jazzy fill on the trumpet)* 'Ere we all are again, boys & girls. A funny thing 'appened to me on the way to the lumber camp, There was this big Mountie 'oo 'adn't seen a woman for 15 years...

BUSTER - I... I couldn't help myself, honestly. I just had to know...

STINKFOOT - What? About the polar bear wiv its 'ead stuck inna flower-pot?

BUSTER *(apologetically advancing; unwittingly lighting the trunk & Screwy)* I'm sorry. I'm sorry. I was just...

STINKFOOT - Don't worry, son - it's an old one, eh? *(for the first time, he notices Screwy)* Oh my god - what 'ave you done?

BUSTER - It wasn't me. I just had to know. I... had to have the secret. How Soliquisto does it, see? I mean, there's a secret to art, right?

STINKFOOT *(prods Screwy, who falls back in a slump)* - I don't adam & eve it. You've 'alf killed him.

BUSTER - Killed him? *Killed* him?

STINKFOOT *(manically stagy)* - Poor ole Screwy. 'Ee'll never laugh again. Ha. Ha. Ha.

BUSTER - Laugh? But he's not real!

STINKFOOT - 'Course not. It's all in the mind - magic.

BUSTER - But the secret ...

STINKFOOT - There is no secret, yer dozy pillock.

BUSTER - You're lying. You're all lying to me.

Suddenly, and again, the cry of the parrot. Startled, both look up.

A low light has appeared in a balconied window above the stage. In it, Persian Moll is silhouetted reaching into a huge bird's cage. She hooks out the terrified occupant (who reacts with one last despairing screech), and bites off its head. Feathers every-where.

Galvanized, first Stinkfoot, then Buster clamber up the fire escape. Moll, cleaning her whiskers, watches them climb.

MOLL - Come up to serenade me, boys? The moon may be full but I'm still hungry.

STINKFOOT - Moll, you crazy bitch. That was Prince Pollyanna, the Queen of the ruddy Songbirds. You ruined the ruddy act! What will The

Great Soliquisto say?

MOLL - When did we ever care what Uncle Solly said? Let's just say...
I'm changin' the act. From soup - *(with a hiss, she shoves him off balance)* -
to nuts.

*Stinkfoot grabs a rope and swings wildly, but Moll bites into his paw, and with a terrible
snarl he plummets into darkness.*

MOLL *(leaning over to watch him go)* - Bye bye, love. Bye bye, happiness.
(rounds on Buster) And now for you...

BUSTER *(terrified he'll be next)* - Me, Moll?

Clinging to the ladder, he looks down at the still body of Stinkfoot - and so does Moll.

MOLL - What's been hid... ain't been did. Get rid of the stiff. And get rid
of that stupid trumpet too.

BUSTER - But Moll...

MOLL - Just do it!

*Scampering down, Buster opens one of the large dressing room windows (outside
there's a full moon over the midnight sea). Picking up the limp Stinkfoot, he throws him
into the waves. Great splash! Out goes the trumpet. 2nd splash. Offstage, a storm
rumbles & grumbles; there are strange shrieks.*

*Buster, frightened & appalled, stares up in horror at Moll who's been purring to
herself & cleaning her fur.*

MOLL *(points to Screwy)* - Clean him up and get lost - 'til I whistle. Ooo! I
broke a nail.

Stretching and preening, Moll sings:

BAD, BAD WAYS

Now there ain't no cat to look at the Queen,
If I give you the chop, I'm the guillotine.
'Cause, ooo - I got some bad bad ways.

I'm the Queen of the crop, the top of the tree -
I'm tellin' you, baby... don't you mess with me.
'Cause, ooo - I got some bad bad ways.
Bad bad ways, bad bad ways.
(gives out a big throaty, catty laugh)

Kill light in window. Which leaves a stunned Buster centre stage.

Blackout.

ACT ONE, SCENE TWO.

The foreshore beach under the pier. Night & the full fat moon. Mournful tolling of solemn bells, raven croaks, deep foghorns, and the sounds of surf. Lit red by a swinging storm lantern, looms the face of a Coastguard, sou'westered & singing. On the beach & throughout, erotically, exotically, dance three shadowy Woeful Sirens.

THRENODY – STINKFOOT IS DROWNED

COASTGUARD - Stinkfoot is drowned!
ALL - Oh, let us mourn him!
COASTGUARD - Stinkfoot is drowned!
MOLL *(offstage)* - Where is my love?
COASTGUARD - Rotting on the bottom of the dustbin sea!
ALL - Stinkfoot is drowned! Stinkfoot is drowned!
COASTGUARD - Stinkfoot is dead! Stinkfoot is dead!
MOLL *(offstage)* - Stinkfoot will never be found.
ALL - Stinkfoot was carried away by the sea.
COASTGUARD - Stinkfoot is dead!
ALL - Oh, let us mourn!
COASTGUARD - Down amongst the dead things, dead things dead!

MOLL *(offstage)* - Rotting on the bottom of the dustbin sea-ea-ea-ea-ea!
COASTGUARD - Isn't it a tragedy when life so brief & beautiful,
is snatched away, and dashed away, and swallowed by the sea.
Where is all his funeral, and where the purple pageantry? Bah!
ALL - *(taunting)* Nah. Nah. Nah. Nah. Nah.
COASTGUARD - Oh, this is vilest obliquity...
ALL - We don't understand you.
COASTGUARD - I don't expect brass knobs on it, but where is your respect?
Stinkfoot is *dead*!

The Coastguard & voices fade while the dancing Sirens sink to the sand and slither away. Lights dim even further until all is penumbral. A musical crossfade, SURE AS EGGS IS EGGS, rouses the atmosphere as a large spot picks out the theatrical trunk - and an empty wheelchair.
Enter a tap dancing Soliquisto. (His Shadow is danced by the black figured Stinkfoot. At the music's climax, Stinkfoot is gone.)
Soliquisto bows to the audience, pulls Screwy from the trunk (the dummy has a livid scar on its forehead), then seats himself in the wheelchair. Screwy on his knee, he addresses both dummy & audience.

SOLIQUISTO *(brightly, but resignedly)* - Nine long years. Where does the time go? But oh, when Stinkfoot died, it broke my heart! Of course, they called it a stroke. Lost the use of my legs. Didn't dance anymore. Well, I couldn't, could I? *(points to lettering on the trunk)* Oh, I was great once and so were my friends. And that was the thing of it - To be with my friends. But what can an artist do, eh Screwy?
SCREWY - Just grin and bear it. Bear and grin it. Show 'em what you're made of! Carry on. Ooooh! What a carry on!
SOLIQUISTO - So I carried on. Without, I suppose you'd say - Without... well, with a bit of me missing.
SCREWY - 'Ere, 'ere, 'ere. I've seen you in the showers and a knob's as good as a winkle...
SOLIQUISTO - Stop that. It's... filthy. You could go blind.
SCREWY - Can't I do it a little bit - and wear glasses?
SOLIQUISTO - Stop that or back in the box with you! *(to audience)* All I could do was carry on. Blackpool, Scarboro', Southend, Cardiff, Rhyll, Clacton... and poor old Screwy. He never really got over that awful

maniac's attack on his head. Never did find out who did it.
(to Screwy) Didn't get over it, did you?

SCREWY *(leering, half crazed)* - Never got over it, no! Not if I live to be a thousand... and oh! The pain and the shame. And the boo-hoo-hoo miliation. *(smartly)* But did I have a choice? I did. Yes! So I carried on!

SOLIQUISTO - Yes, we carried on. With myself crippled and you schizophrenic!

SCREWY - It was a split decision.

SOLIQUISTO - I had half a mind to give it all up.

SCREWY - I just had half a mind.

TOGETHER *(sweetly)* - But we carried on.
(very politely) - Do you mind not talking while I'm talking?
(accusingly) - I'm not talking while you're talking ...
(angrily) - You're talking while I'm talking!
(pause) - I...
(huffily) - I saw your lips move!

SOLIQUISTO - So we carried on - for nine long years. From one end-of-the pier to another. Seaside. Westside.

SCREWY - Seaside. Seesaws. Don't mention saws!

SOLIQUISTO - Ramsgate, Brighton, Torquay... and now back here to...

SCREWY - *Where* did you say we were, Sir?

SOLIQUISTO - Does it matter anymore, where we are? Here we are again!
(sadly) But yes, it matters. *Here* is where I found Stinkfoot.
(laughs) Oh! And Moll of course. But Stinkfoot, well...

SCREWY - A very remarkable animal, Sir! And a credit to you, Sir! A living testament to the - Soliquisto School of Training, Sir!

SOLIQUISTO - Stinkfoot! What a pupil! Never missed a trick.
(music under: LANDING ON MY FEET FEET) Stinkfoot took to 'The Show Business' like a...

SCREWY - Starving animal, Sir?

SOLIQUISTO *(ignores that)* - When I found them, Stinkfoot and Moll were just stray cats begging for scraps under the pier when the tide was out. *(laughs)* They used to follow that mad woman with the bags 'til they came to live with me. Remember?

SCREWY - If you say so, Sir!

SOLIQUISTO - I wonder if she's still down there - under the pier. With her bags - and her... *(looks at the floor uneasily - then brightens)* You could hear her cats even up here in the dressing room.

SCREWY - Like the wailing of the banshee, Sir - when there's soon to be a death in the house.

SOLIQUISTO *(laughs nervously)* - Oh, nonsense. I used to entice them with salmon. And the noise they made when they heard Prince Pollyanna - Our Queen of Songbirds - sing.

SCREWY *(whistles a snatch of PARAKEET TO MEET YOU)*

(impatiently) - All very well, but where are we?

SOLIQUISTO *(dreamily)* - I was thinking of Stinkfoot and some of the old routines.

Looking at each other in sudden enthusiasm, Soliquisto & Screwy spring up into an 'old routine'. Soliquisto still has his hand up the back of the dancing Screwy. In two follow spots there is much excitement! & snappy business! Routine winds down in slo mo until Screwy falls to the floor & only Soliquisto's face is lit.

SOLIQUISTO *(wearily & sadly)* - Ah, well. On with my painted face to face the unvarnished reality... It is so sweet for a man to dream.

Fade to Blackout. The stage is dark for a second, then...

BUSTER *(offstage hiss-whisper)* - Moll! Moll! Moll, I have an idea... Moll, I know you're listening. You're always listening. Moll?

Offstage sinister hiss.

ACT ONE,
SCENE THREE.

Dawn under the pier. For the first time, the stage is fully lit. A vast seashore-scape. Mist on the sea and roseate light. Pier-piling seaweedy & dripping. Quiet but for the whisper of surf. The tide is a long way out and the beach is strewn with trash & a bijouterie of shimmering rock pools. Grim cocklesheds smoke ominously amidst the explosive sounds of hissing and sudden bubbling.

Completely flat and half-covered in sand, stage right, is Isaiah, the Flounder, snoring. (We can hear him, but not actually see him.) Perched on top of a nearby half-rotted piling is the sleeping Polly, the Foundling Budgerigar, head under her wing. Twined round with kelp, stage left, Elma, the Electrifying Elver, yawns & preens. Somewhere in the background, wanders the Balanced Nose.

From offstage comes the contended humming (music: SPHINX & MINX) of Mrs Bag Bag. She enters, weighted down with many & various bags, poking in rock pools, stooping and squinting in wonderment - only to trip up on the half-buried Isaiah.

MRS BAG BAG *(singing)* - What can I hide so deep inside Me bag, bag, bag, bag, bag, bag, bag? - Oops! *(speaks)* What's this? What's this? Is it something for me bags?

The music segues into YOU CAN'T CONFOUND A FLOUNDER as she pokes him in the eye.

ISAIAH *(flopping around like the flatfish he is)* - Oh dear! dear, dear... dear, dear... dear dear. Oh, dear! dear dear... dear dear... dear.

ELMA *(slithering over to peer into Mrs Bag Bag's bags)* - Grumble, grumble, grumble, etc. Glum!

No longer interested, Mrs Bag Bag is off to poke at something else. But the commotion awakens Polly and she spreads her colourful wings in a huge stretching yawn.

POLLY - Confused again, Isaiah?

Struggling to his 'feet', helped by The Balanced Nose, Isaiah groans into:

YOU CAN'T CONFOUND A FLOUNDER

ISAIAH - Oh no! Oh no! You can't confound a flounder
'cos a flounder knows what's what.
From lyin' on the bottom and lookin' around a lot.
You can't expect a cynic
To be other than what he is.
Findin' fault with everything - oh, isn't life a swizz?
ALL - Oh dear dear dear... dear dear dear dear!
ISAIAH - Life is just a muddle... and I live in a puddle,
and all that I presume - is gloom.
ALL - Grumble, grumble... etc.
MRS BAG BAG - When you look at life askance,
you simply haven't got a chance. Give up!
ISAIAH - Dear, dear, dear... oh, dear dear.
ALL - Dear, dear, dear... oh, dear dear. Give up!

ISAIAH *(speaks, vastly lugubrious)* - Oh, I am ugly! A real eyesore.
POLLY *(head cocked to one side)* - Ever thought it's the way you look at things?
ISAIAH *(huffily)* - I can't help that, can I?
POLLY - There's times I don't know whether I'm coming or going.
ISAIAH *(speaks)* - Don't worry - you're going. We're *all* going. What a life!

(sings) Oh, dear... dear, dear... dear dear... dear dear.
ALL - Grumble, grumble, grumble, grumble, grumble, etc.

ELMA - When you've got two dodgy minces,
no more frogs turn into princes.
ISAIAH - And I'm boss-eyed beside the sea - GIVE UP! - side.
ALL - GIVE UP! GIVE UP!
ISAIAH - Am I right or am I wrong?
ALL - GIVE UP! GIVE UP!
ISAIAH - It'll all be over soon.
ALL - Give up! Give up!
ISAIAH - Can you hear a cynical song?
ALL - Give up! Give up!
ISAIAH (spoken, not sung) - Admit defeat! Everything is grey or brown!
Apologize! Whine. Cower & frown. Abandon hope!
If things could be worse - they will.
Just feed & breed! And wallow in your swill!
(points at audience) Your life has no meaning - think of it:
A vast unbounded bottomless pit! Ha! Ha! Ha!
Give up. It's not complicated.
ALL (low & hissing) - Give up.

Isaiah mutters off. But Polly stands on her piling in an effort to fly. Much flapping. Behind her, Elma makes faces... ignored, she insinuates herself into one of Mrs Bag Bag's bags.

MRS BAG BAG - Polly, dear. What's a feather for? Fly! Fly!

Polly flaps harder - & Awk-squawk! suddenly pitches forward. With a thump, she lands behind a cockleshed. (Puff of feathers.) When she emerges, she looks shamefaced & shaken.
Meanwhile, an unconcerned Mrs Bag Bag has plopped down onto the sand & buried her head in another of her 'magic' bags. (Note: In these bags there might be anything: any one, or two, or more, of which Mrs B. extracts whenever it suits her.)

POLLY (humbly) - I'll never learn. I do it all wrong. (looks down at herself, feathers everywhichway) I look all wrong too.
ELMA (from inside a bag) - All wrong is dead right, all right.
MRS BAG BAG (from inside her bag) - Once a thing's in me bags - it's in its proper place.

ISAIAH (gloomily) - I'm an improper plaice. Ha. Ha. But do I feel happy? Two wrongs don't make a right... but - (he puts his fin around Polly & looks lewdly hopeful) Three do! (deflated when Polly shrugs him off) It's not worth the bother. Am I right? Or am I wrong?

POLLY - I'll never give up. Not until I find out who I am.

ELMA (oozing out from the bag & full of scorn) - I know who you are. You're...

POLLY - Nobody. Nobody at all! No mum. No dad. No family tree. All I've got is Mrs Bag Bag.

Polly looks down lovingly at the humming rummaging bag and sings:

A FOUNDLING'S SONG, or BORN IN A BAG

If I had the confidence,
The courage or the common sense,
The chutzpah or some happiness -
Then I could face the future.
If I could find a kindred spirit,
Wouldn't mind a friend to share it -
For I'm the thing with feathers that perches in the soul.

All that's second-best in me
Is crying out for sympathy, and nagging insecurity
is begging me: don't try!

But if I am to know myself,
And if I am to grow myself,
Then I must just let go myself,
And fear must say its prayers.

If there were an easier way, a magic I could try...
Or someone else to do this thing for me,
But fear must say its prayers - Tonight!

Isaiah slumps more and more as Polly sings. Mrs Bag Bag has come out of her bag, munching something forever unknown. But Elma has slithered into a dance of cocky confidence. At 'Tonight!', she dives into the sea.
Comes a great clap of thunder and a Shining Spot centre stage. All collapse.

VOICE OF GOD *(gently)* - Don't Give Up. Regard this man. He is very drowned and yet flooded with life.

Lights dim, thunder rumbles, lightning cracks, and out of the pin-spotted sea comes the Drowned Sailor, followed by an awed Elma (in her own pin spot). She is singing:

DROWNED SAILOR'S DREAM

I sing to you as a siren sweetly sings!
I sing to you of a love harmonious & deep.
Be with me - sailor.
Come to me - sailor. Here I am - sailor.

I sing to you as a diver arc-ing deep!
I sing to you of a secret only you can keep.
Be with me - sailor.
Come to me - sailor. Here I am - sailor.

Sea-wives sing of sailors... sailors far from home.
Lovers dream of lovers. Never more alone!
Sing ho for rescue! Sing ho.

The Drowned Sailor stands dripping & rotten, centre stage.
God laughs. And the laughter is segued with deep sea gurgles. These sea sounds punctuate all that follows.

DROWNED SAILOR - Oh! I am drowned and yet flooded with life.
ISAIAH - Oh, 'ee's drowned, all right.
DROWNED SAILOR - I am soaked with sensation - drenched with senses.

ISAIAH - 'E's soaked to the skin. Pro'bly 'ad a skinful.

DROWNED SAILOR - And I will tell you everything you need to know - deep secrets of the deep.

POLLY *(coming forward to touch him, but can't make herself)* - I have things I need to know...

ISAIAH *(coming forward to urge Polly away, though she does not budge)* - I wish I could forget the things I know.

MRS BAG BAG *(coming forward to collect bits off the sailor and pop them in her bags)* - I keeps all I knows safe in me bags.

ELMA *(coming forward to twine herself around the sailor)* - I dive. I know all about the hot, deep, guilty places.

Mrs Bag Bag grabs the Drowned Sailor's hand, only to have his skin slough off. Eeeeuuu! go All... and everyone backs away at once. That too goes in her bag... as the Drowned Sailor begins to walk back towards the sea.

POLLY - You said you would tell us secrets!

DROWNED SAILOR - When I died, I was not a bit myself! And yet - I was wholly me.

POLLY *(desperately)* - Died? Death? But I want answers about Life!

DROWNED SAILOR - Where is the difference? It doesn't really matter.

Music (NO TIME LIKE THE FUTURE) softly building under... and up comes a full moon to sail slowly across the sky.

ISAIAH *(very sadly & looking only at Polly)* - Some things matter rather a lot to me.

VOICE OF GOD - In the beginning there was no matter. But that doesn't matter.

As Polly and Isaiah begin their duet (Mrs Bag Bag & Elma as backup), the Drowned Sailor is hoisted (as if in ascension) up past the moon & into darkness.

NO TIME LIKE THE FUTURE

POLLY, MRS BAG BAG & ELMA - The moon follows, the old patterns are taking place in the sky...
POLLY - Here am I, filled with wonder.
ISAIAH - But I'm crying.
POLLY, MRS BAG BAG, & ELMA - The sea follows the moon patterns, the waves whisper to tides. Change is the whole of your life...
ISAIAH - Keep on rolling.
POLLY - You say there is no time like the future. But now's the time...
POLLY & ISAIAH - Now's the time.
ISAIAH - But I'm still looking forward to what used to be -
POLLY & ISAIAH - But now's the time,
ALL - Now's the time.
ISAIAH - Come to me, baby - I'm sick and I'm tired.
My mind is in the way of my light -
And I can't see the wrong from the right.
And I'm crying.
Without you, I'm here.
I'm out there, I'm howling -
I love you, but I'm alone.
You say: follow me home -
And I'm flying.

Blackout

ACT ONE, SCENE FOUR.

In the Blackout, Buster's voice is sudden, fierce - loudly demanding.

BUSTER - Are you listening, uncle?

Lights up to reveal the tawdry backstage dressing room of the End-of-the-Pier Pavilion. Offstage, there is laughter & applause and the badly miked voice of a compere indistinctly announcing an act. Comes clapping & music (NICE & TIDY) which fades but still punctuates the following action.
Only the naked bulbs around the dressing tables of Soliquisto & Buster illuminate the scene. In his wheelchair, a distracted Soliquisto faces his mirror (facing the audience). Buster, in a silly cat costume, whiskers painted on his face, busies himself with Screwy and his props. A piano, a painted screen, and the travelling trunk decorate the room. Behind, the open windows look out upon a moonlit sea.

SOLIQUISTO - Yes, I hear things.
BUSTER - Then listen to this... when I have an *idea*, it crackles!
SOLIQUISTO *(hopeful for this one moment)* - Really?
BUSTER *(excitedly removing make-up)* - You gotta picture it, see? It's a
    crackeroo. Venice is sinking!
SOLIQUISTO *(lighting a cigarette & looking at his sad surroundings - sounds of sea)*
    (hope flown again) - Yes, I can imagine that.
BUSTER *(miming awkwardly)* - There's this old tap dancer in the gutter...
SOLIQUISTO - Bojangles?
BUSTER *(seriously)* - Eh? Bo... jangles? Uh. I suppose he could, yes. Anyway,

the girl is a kind of orphan - but what *she* doesn't know is...

From behind a False Tab, Moll's face pops out and smirks.

MOLL - That she's really a toad.

Soliquisto smiles at her with immense pride. Hissing, she's gone.

BUSTER - No. That she's the daughter of a Russian sword-swallower - and that's where she gets the big voice.
SOLIQUISTO *(bored, but sympathetic)* - A Romanoff, perhaps?
BUSTER - Not a gypsy, no. Just an orphan.
SCREWY *(still slumped crazily on the floor)* - Is she orphan on? Or on and orf? Orf for one and one for orff? Get orff!
BUSTER *(grasping Screwy and shaking him)* - Shut up!

Buster drags Screwy to the piano bench where Screwy launches into SONG OF THE SAW, and crack-voicedly sings.

SCREWY - Chop, chop, the red knives drop...
The scraping song of the saw.
Slice, slice, the manikin mice -
Let's bite out more and more!
We weighed it up & we made our decision:
We'd make a teeny weenie incision.
If they find out, we'll all go to prison -
so meanwhile let's enjoy.
(Buster comes close to strangling him)
- arrrrk!
BUSTER *(fiercely)* - I wish you'd stop doing that, Uncle Solly. It gives me the creeps.

Screwy slumps as soon as Soliquisto looks in his direction.

SOLIQUISTO - I do beg your pardon, my boy. The mind does begin to adventure a little... after a certain age. And, well - perhaps it's just being back here. I can't stop believing... *(turns sadly to the window)* that at any instant...

BUSTER *(furiously upset)* - Yes! Yes! Stinkfoot will make one of his famous bloody funny entrances - rattlin' his chains and jugglin' his balls. Well, he's gone. Buggered off and left you years ago. By now, he's dead, I reckon. *(offstage laughter & applause)* Dead. Drowned. Brown bread. Dead. And now there's just you and me. You've got to start thinking about me. About us. I'm good. I've got it. You taught me, like you taught them. You think I can't be as good as... one of your... *(gestures angrily at Screwy)* things! D'you hear the laughs I got tonight? Big laughs. You think I don't work? You think... *(pause, then with finality)* Stinkfoot is dead.

Buster looks at Screwy who's staring at him, and reacts as though accused. He throws his comically big cat's feet across the dressing room. Soliquisto is gazing deep into his mirror. (Which means right through the audience.)

BUSTER *(sadly)* - What do you see, Uncle?
SCREWY *(hollow as a drum)* - Stinkfoot. Stinkfoot. Stinkfoot!
SOLIQUISTO *(seriously)* - I see myself a long time ago. And hope. And fame and the tarnish of too much applause. I'm tired.

Offstage comes tumultuous applause. Calls of MORE! ENCORE! MOLL! In sweeps a triumphant Persian Moll.

MOLL *(hisses)* - You two still talkin' about Stinkfoot?

As Buster keeps out her way, discarding his cat costume, Soliquisto rises in admiration of his creation.

SOLIQUISTO - Moll, I've written something for you... and I rather hoped we could ...
MOLL *(suspicious)* - A new routine for me?
SOLIQUISTO *(pathetically eager)* - Why yes! Something that could get us back...

He is going to say 'back to the Big Time' and Buster knows it... listening, he is helpless in his hurt.

MOLL - Besides starring me, would this new routine have you in it?
SOLIQUISTO - Well, yes... but...
MOLL - Forget it. When I fly, I fly solo. Out there... under the lights - It's

just me and my talent. That's all I got - and it's mine! *(strides to the front of the stage to sing)*

OW! OW! WASN'T I GOOD TONIGHT!

No! I refuse to give my love to anyone.
You'll only die loving me.
And I've been abused for so long, I don't feel your pain.
Yeah, yeah, baby, no more sympathy.
Gimme some lights and a stage and a band
or an orchestra...
And I'm sittin' smug as the Duchess of Muck at the Dorchestra -
Candelabras, fireflies, a stage for me is any size.
So don't psychoanalyse me, apotheosize me!
'Cause, oh baby, wasn't I good -
Ah, honey, did what I should -
Ow! Ow! Baby! Wasn't I good tonight!

Moll shoves Buster out of her way as she takes herself behind the painted screen. Her stage costume is then thrown piece by glittery piece over the top of it.
  It is obvious that Buster won't even glance at Moll. Picking up the dummy from the piano bench, he flops it on his knee.

BUSTER - Trouble with you is *(fiercely)* you're schizophrenic, aren't you, eh? *(tries to work the dummy but Screwy says nothing; Buster shakes it until both their teeth chatter.)* Aren't you? Aren't you!

But just as Buster decides to fling the dummy off, Screwy manically sits erect.

SCREWY - Well, half of me want to say - yes, yes, yes... And the other half wants to say: a gottle of geer - am I right?
SOLIQUISTO *(sunk, once again, in his wheelchair)* *(tiredly)* Leave him alone... he's not real.

BUSTER *(pained)* - Well, who is? Who's who here, Uncle? We're all in the same boat!

SCREWY - Yeah, but some of us ain't got both oars in the water.

SOLIQUISTO - Screwy's right. Balance is tantamount to health.

BUSTER *(dropping Screwy)* - Health? Health! My genius is starving. You won't give me a chance.

SOLIQUISTO - It is only to give you your 'chance' - to allow you choice, that is, that I have 'protected' you, if you like!

BUSTER - I don't like. Oh hell, how long am I gonna be just your ruddy assistant? You don't want to listen - you're too damn busy listening to yourself. *(suddenly rueful)* I'm sorry, Uncle. *(brightly)* Look, I got a great idea for a new routine - put this in your pigeon loft and see if it carries any messages.

SCREWY - It'll be a stinkerooonie!

The dummy has begun dragging itself to the piano. Half in fear, Buster abruptly stands.

BUSTER - No, listen. It's got life and laffs - and real human values. It'll sell. It's really wild.

SOLIQUISTO *(quite seriously)* - I know that wildness. I was wild myself, once. Until that time, I was wild with joy.

As Screwy climbs up on the piano bench, Buster drops to his knees beside his uncle.

BUSTER - I've even written a song. A real show stopper. *(Screwy pounds out a few discordant chords and Buster croons)* Don't cry for me, Idi Amin-a...

SCREWY *(singing smarmily)* - It's too late to thaa-aaw the fridge!

Horrified, Soliquisto looks at his nephew, but harder and longer at Screwy.

SOLIQUISITO - That's... disturbingly familiar. And derivative.

Dressed for a night on the razzle, Persian Moll sidles from behind the screen, and postures.

MOLL *(sarcastic)* - You still preachin', Uncle Solly?

SOLIQUISTO *(reflectively)* - I suppose the whole of my work is a kind of confession.

MOLL - Well bless me, Father - god knows, I've sinned a few times myself.

Exit Persian Moll, scratching a red streak in the wall as she goes.

BUSTER *(checks to make sure Moll is gone)* - What's past is past.
SOLIQUISTO - The past is a foreign country, they do things differently there.
SCREWY - Leave it out, Solly. Leave it out.
BUSTER *(puts his arm around Soliquisto's shoulders)* - We could be in the big time again. Moll's talent. Your connections. My ideas.
SOLIQUISTO *(sadly)* - I know your greed. I was in love, once - with myself. And I hungered for more and more of it.
BUSTER - You don't need no Stinkfoots. You got the lot. And with me...! If only you'd let me in on your... well, The Secret. I mean, I can do everything you can do, almost. It's the other bit, you know. *(glances at the dummy with its livid chopped wood scar, glances away)* What is it? I can't seem to...
SOLIQUISTO - You poor boy. You really do think there's a secret - something I keep to myself. Something I won't let you have... and yet I'm trying to give it to you all the time. But you're too... too...
SCREWY *(horribly)* - Ordinary?
SOLIQUISTO & BUSTER - Shut up!
SOLIQUISTO - ... too anxious to take it. Too worked up all the time about the surface of things, and not about the things that *really* matter. Audiences sense this.
SCREWY *(taps its gashed wooden head)* - They know, you know.
BUSTER - You want to know what I know? What I know is that we've been traipsing round these filthy seaside dumps for bloody donkey's years - and I'm sick of it. Where am I going? *(turns to Screwy)* If you say back to Southend! *(again to Soliquisto)* What's in it for me? I'm brilliant. All you have to do is 'pass it on' or something. Listen. This is right up your street.

Buster sings QUICKCHANGE ARTISTE accompanied on the piano throughout by Screwy.

QUICKCHANGE ARTISTE

In between the headline acts performed a Quickchange Artiste,
While the compere turned his back to 'ave a beer.
And as the Quickchange Artiste was pushin' sixty-plus -
He tried to make a comeback - but 'e'd been nowhere.
Well, his wife she played piano for the Quickchange Artiste,
While the poor ole bugger did his stuff.
He ducked behind a screen and be-come Bill Sykes, then Nancy -
Then quicker than a flash - he was someone else!
Well, his wife would feign surprise at all his engaging little tricks,
While the poor ole bugger did his stuff.
Falling about, falling apart, funny - then sad,
Wiv his hand on his heart.
And the climax was (x 3) - was when his bloomin' wig fell off!
And the climax was, was when 'is bloomin' wig fell off!
Oh! Where *does* a Quickchange Artiste go?
Same verse. Different words!
Wiv his hand stuck up his shirt he be-come Quasimodo,
At which point his painted wife she played the bells.
(Ding dong!)
In the winter of his discontent, he dropped down on his knees.
(drops to his knees)
And pitifully he began to yell:
Look at me. I've filled the stage with faces. Look at me.
There's nothing left.
Look at me, in me shirt and braces. Look at me.
Can you hear me, Mother? Look at me. At me.
I run a damn good race, but now there's nothing left.
Look at me! I filled the stage with faces... but look at me!

Buster 'dies' tragically. With big stagy gestures.

BUSTER *(from the floor, exhausted)* - Is that what you want? Pretty corny, isn't
it?

SOLIQUISTO *(shaken)* - The truth usually is.

BUSTER *(shrugs & gets up)* - Oh, dear... now we're going to talk about 'The Showbusiness'. Or will it be Art? All I'm talking about is getting something out of this that's real. A little bit of comfort, maybe. But you keep the secret from me.

SOLIQUISTO *(looking in his mirror, but addressing the audience)* - It's a terrible thing not to be able to share what you call The Secret. I want you to know - honestly, I do. Especially now that Stinkfoot's gone.

BUSTER - You're not telling me a bloody dancing cat understood it - but I *don't*!

SOLIQUISTO *(while Screwy acts out JOY as acrobatically as possible)* - But he did know. That's why Stinkfoot was so important to me. He was the breathing personification of everything I was too frightened to do myself. He was marvellous. He breathed life. He radiated it. Everything I believed - there on the stage! He had no fear. He did know! He didn't need to find out. He sensed it!

BUSTER - What? With his whiskers? I dunno what you're on about.

SOLIQUISTO *(sadly)* - I know you don't. It's to do with the tightrope. It's...

SCREWY - It's all in the mind.

BUSTER - You're getting old. You won't let me take over. You don't think I'm...

SCREWY - A real artist?

From offstage, softly, drifts the music of NO TIME LIKE THE FUTURE.

SOLIQUISTO *(addressing the air)* - No time like the future? I'll be with you shortly - I just have to live through this lot.

GOD *(offstage, low but audible)* - Oh, no you don't.

SOLIQUISTO - Oh, yes I do! *(to Buster, who reacts with horror)* I know what you did.

BUSTER - You can't know. You weren't there. It wasn't...

SCREWY - It wasn't *me*, Sir.

SOLIQUISTO *(gently but firmly)* - I know. *(looks directly at the audience, finding one face, then another)* Whatever the secret is, I've had it since I was a child. I just didn't know what I was like wasn't true for other people. In a way, that was a mistake of innocence. To despair is easy, to hope is hard - and that's because optimism is creative. And, unlike greed - there is no prescription. *(Screwy comes in on piano)* It's all instinctual, really.

Suddenly, Soliquisto bounds from his wheelchair, full of life & dance & 'tricks' & The Secret. With the backing of an offstage Chorus, he sings:

FOLLOW YOUR NOSE

I used to take advice from other people,
I used to think: just everybody knows...
(whatever it is) - but not me!
I never thought I could do a bally thing right,
But nowadays: I follow my nose! My nose!
I used to get the shits about the future,
And everyday I'd read my horoscope,
Until my nose told me: whatever suits yer
is okey-doke, so follow your nose.
Nowadays I'm ruled by intuition,
I rely upon my spirit guide. I'd love to say that I'd
reasoned how? And reasoned why?
But I'd never trust my nose, altho' I tried, I tried!
Too hard! And oh, what a ninny
I was to think my head could rule my heart.
I'd rather be myself than be Houdini...
That's the secret of my life -
But is it Art? Aha!
Now I have a nose that I can follow,
And nobody can lead me by the nose.
And if you've never tried Sixth Sense -
(offstage Chorus) - Oh, poo!
It's nice & airy in the gents.
Where I used to sit and wonder why... oh, why?
I used to get the shits about the future,
And everyday I'd read my horoscope -
Until my nose told me: don't be a moocher,
Get off your bum and follow your nose.

During the last verse, which plays slower & slower, Soliquisto moves back into his wheelchair. There, he seems to be listening to something under the floor, and he smiles.

BUSTER *(eager, moving props, not yet noticing)* - Okay! I think I get it. Let's go to work. I've been blocking out this idea for me and... well, mostly me. It's about a tobacco baron who breeds sparrows in his cell - Uncle, are you listening?

Rising in volume, below pier noises, Mrs Bag Bag crooning SPHINX & MINX, euphonium whales & surf.

SOLIQUISTO - Oh, yes.
BUSTER - You're *not* listening! Uncle?

Dead Blackout
save for the music of SPHINX & MINX.

ACT ONE, SCENE FIVE.

The sea as seen from under the foot of the pier. Comes the yawning pink-streamered dawn to reveal a beach littered with interesting debris. Three large hollow barnacles hunker wherever, and there is a drift of smoke from the cocklesheds.
Enter Mrs Bag Bag bent under the weight of her bags as she collects & catalogues her tiny treasures.

SPHINX & MINX

Here a hat pin, here a welly -
Doubtless from the Kraken's belly!
Here a wishbone - make a wish:
I wish you'd all stop hurting fish!
Here a float and here a hook,
Do let me have another look.
What can I hide so deep inside
Me bag, bag, bag, bag, bag, bag, bag?

Little things unloved & lost,
Little things I do accost.
Little things grow bigger in me bag, bag, bag, bag.
Wakey! Wakey!

Does it make you feel uneasy,
Knowing that I'm going crazy?
Fingers like a busy lizzie,
Busy in me bag, bag, bag, bag.

She raps smartly on a large barnacle.

MRS BAG BAG - I know you're in there!

The barnacle slowly rolls over to reveal a sleepy, yawning, stretching Elma. Mrs Bag Bag rudely pokes her.

ELMA *(pushing her hand away)* - Stop it! Go away! No. No! Damn! You have broken my dream. *(to dream)* Oh, come back! Come back! Where was I? Where is it? Gone... all gone. *(glares around her)* I do not like Mrs Bag Bag. I do not like real life.
MRS BAG BAG - Get up, you lazy fish. Mrs Bag Bag wants you to dive into the deep. *(points out to sea)* The bags tell me... there is *something*... out there - to keep.

Erotically & snap-crackle-sparking, Elma wriggles out under from the barnacle.

ELMA - You Bag Bag Bag! If I were not so bored, I would shock you.
MRS BAG BAG *(dreamily looking out to sea, not really listening)* - Nothing ever shocks me, dear. I've seen it all, seen it all. What goes down, comes up. What goes round, gets dizzy. *(rustles & rattles her bags)* Fill them up. Fill them up. What comes home - comes sooner than you think.

Elma languidly begins to climb one of the sea-weedy pilings of the pier.

ELMA *(sullen)* - I do not think - I dive. And I fzzzzttt-spit-crackle. It is what I *do* - and I do it very well. But what the hell do I do it *for*?

Climbing straight up, she disappears from view, and a second later on dashes a Partly Cooked Shrimp. He is steaming & hysterical.

PARTLY COOKED SHRIMP - They're trying to cook me, Missus! Help me -

I'm half done already. *(glancing fearfully behind him, he tries to clamber into Mrs Bag Bag's biggest bag)* Sanctuary - I beg you!

MRS BAG BAG - Out! Out! Out! Your time hasn't come yet.

PARTLY COOKED SHRIMP - Oh, yes it has. Oh! The cauldrons. The terrible boiling cauldrons. And the shrieks of the lobsters!

MRS BAG BAG - Shrieks? No, no. They're singing. Go away.

PARTLY COOKED SHRIMP - I can't! I can't! Hide me.

There is the sound of a large splash as Elma dives into the sea. She appears middle distance among the waves - swimming out.

PARTLY COOKED SHRIMP - Oh, no. There goes another poor devil.

MRS BAG BAG *(digs something silly out of a bag, and goes for him with it)* - That was just a naughty eel - *go away!*

PARTLY COOKED SHRIMP - Oh my god! They keeps the eels alive for days, Keeps 'em on ice. Then, *then*, they chops 'em up alive.

MRS BAG BAG *(almost interested)* - Do they?

PARTLY COOKED SHRIMP - It's horrible, horrible! What have I done? *(he clasps his claws)* Hail Mary, full of gravy, tartar sauce over thee, Boiled art thou amongst lobsters.

Out at sea, a laughing Elma comes up from a dive, blowing a trumpet.

PARTLY COOKED SHRIMP *(startled by blast)* - They're coming for me. Arggghhhh!

He dashes off, pursued by a Horrid Cockler.

MRS BAG BAG *(to audience)* - Always Mrs Bag Bag, harbouring by the sea.
Suns and moons time-keeping by - but what do I keep by me?
Peep into Mrs Bag Bag's bags, where the secrets are asleep.
Busy Mrs Bag Bag knows the secrets of the deep.

Enter Polly and Isaiah. Isaiah, wearing sunglasses, is immensely proud to have Polly on his armfin. Polly wears her Sunday best bonnet and carries an umbrella. During the following 'music hall' exchange, Elma swims happily about in the sea with the trumpet.

POLLY - There you are, Mrs Bag Bag. We've been in town.

ISAIAH - And me, knowing how much Polly wants to fly, well, I slipped into a chemist's, and...

POLLY (surprised) - You did?

ISAIAH - Indeed, I did. I slipped into a chemist's and got you some oint-ment, dear. And a fly. (produces a jar) It's called a Flyin' the Ointment. Har. Har. Har.

Suddenly, out at sea, Elma is attacked by a Giant Squid. Holding up speech balloons that say: EEK! and Help, oh! HELP!, she struggles & goes under. Just then, a deep-throated foghorn announces the arrival of an Ocean Liner on the far horizon. There is a tiny figure dancing on the deck.

POLLY (pulling on the laughing Flounder's fin & pointing out to sea) - Good grief! Look, Isaiah! Out there. A young life is in danger!

ISAIAH (with a great show of manly concern) - Hold up!

This, Mrs Bag Bag cannot ignore. Is it something for her bag? Ready for anything, she pulls out a huge butterfly net from the largest - and waits with interest.

Elma goes down one more time in the tentacles of the Squid. The Ocean Liner bristles with speech balloons: HAVE NO FEAR! I SHALL RESCUE YOU! WHEN YOU WALK THROUGH A STORM. BE THERE IN A JIFFY! COMING!

The little figure on the deck dives overboard. It is Stinkfoot who now swims strongly for Elma, as, accompanied by All, Isaiah (watching with a sense of 'any moment now' going out to help), sings:

SHARKS OF MECHANICAL TIME

ISAIAH - Hold up!

ALL - Ho!

ISAIAH - A young life is in danger. Sing strong!

ALL - Ho!

ISAIAH (softly) - What else can we do? (loudly) Sing strong. Swim strong.

ALL - Pull.

ISAIAH - And pull her here to safety. Swim strong.

For the sharks of mechanical time

ALL - Are biting each soft second
ISAIAH - Away!
ISAIAH - And we may be too late...
ALL - Oh no!
ISAIAH - And who pray?
ALL - Ave!
ISAIAH - Will volunteer to save her? Who pray?
ALL (softly) - Who pray...
ISAIAH - No, no, not me! Pooh! Aye, aye.
ALL - Ohhhh!
ISAIAH - I spy a bold young hearty! Aye. Aye.
ALL - Ohhh!
ISAIAH - He will rescue she! Swim strong.
ALL - Pull!
ISAIAH - Oh god, I hates a volunteer-o!
ALL - Swim strong!
POLLY - Good grief! A giant squid has grabbed her!
ALL - Good grief.
ISAIAH - Well, go on - and pull its bloomin' head off.
ALL - Pull!

After much struggling in the tentacles of the Squid, Stinkfoot and Elma have now reached shore. He strikes a heroic stance, then notices the Squid still has the trumpet, so back he goes to rescue that. Once more, he strikes a heroic stance, holding his trumpet aloft. Like kelp, Elma drapes herself over him.

ELMA *(crackling)* - Is he not a hero!

Mrs Bag Bag, usually so unconcerned, takes one look at the 'hero', & hides herself in a bag. Polly would push forward, but jealous of her awe, Isaiah tries using his great flat body as a shield. Stinkfoot, indulgently untwining Elma from round his neck, leaps amongst them.

STINKFOOT *(now has a New York accent)* - Hiya, cats! Some entrance, huh? Not the way my agent expected... But not bad for the headlines. I can see 'em now. Stinkfoot - that's me! - Returns A hero! Or... or... Stinkfoot - that's me too - Makes A Big Splash! Or... or... *(bumps into*

Isaiah) Sorry, Mack... but why doncha...

ISAIAH *(oozing scorn)* - Why don'choo look where you're going?

STINKFOOT - Why don't he go where he's lookin'?

ELMA *(to audience)* - Did you see him dive? Only I can dive as well as he. It was - masterful.

STINKFOOT - That's true.

ELMA - I dive because I was born to dive. But what is he to dive for me? A catfish!

STINKFOOT - That's true too.

ELMA - Unshell-fish he, and full of spunk.

STINKFOOT - That's true too... pretty much. Wow, I'm gettin' bored with this.

ISAIAH *(to audience)* - I would of been in there meself - but you can't trust these eyes. I most pro'bly would have had *her* head off, and rescued the bloomin' squid.

STINKFOOT *(once more peeling off Elma, he catches sight of Polly)* - Say, I know you. Now, you I know. That is most definitely for certain. You ever work the jungle?

Chords under: THE BIG STIFF.

POLLY - No, I... the jungle?

STINKFOOT - Broadway, kid. Like this... *(stage lights dim to dark, save for a follow spot on Stinkfoot)* I was working in a jungle... hooked on a hunch that made Richard III sound like an entry in a spinster's diary. It was easy. Find the rat in the haystack and the chiggers would pile out of the woods waving their needles. There aren't many crooked streets left in this town a wet cat can walk down with four right legs. Right? But I hadda gedda confession: mea culpa? Maybe. But not as culpa as the killers I'd sent to the chair. 'Will ya scream for me, Rocky? So dat the other kids know ya have a yellow streak in ya?' And before the moon waxed too poetic like something you have to pick out of your ear with a sledgehammer, I was gonna find him. In the jungle!

Lights up, to find all stunned by this rattled-off nonsense. They shake themselves awake.

POLLY - I've never been anywhere but here - have I, Mrs Bag Bag?

MRS BAG BAG *(from inside the bag)* - Oh... I wouldn't say that. Exactly.

47

STINKFOOT - Okay. So you're somebody else already. So who cares? *(to audience)* But I know you. And you know me. Eggy peggy leggy, and I should coco. Okay, let's go! And all that jazz. *(to Polly)* Anyways, you'd be an old old bird by now - nine years? You'd be a turkey. Or a Peking duck. Leastways, a boiler. Fergeddit. *(looks at the lump that is Mrs Bag Bag in her bag)* But say! I'd know that old bag anywhere.

POLLY - You know Mrs Bag Bag?

STINKFOOT - Sure thing, kiddo - since I was a puss-puss. Me an' Moll used to kick her around like she was our mudda. Excuse me, I gotta go post a letter. *(hops over to open Mrs Bag Bag's bag & yell into it)* Hey! Bag Bag! You still workin' the beach?

MRS BAG BAG *(popping her head out of her bag)* - Some people know where home is. And some pussy cats know a birdcage from a handsaw.

During the following Stinkfoot shtick, in dumb show Mrs Bag Bag fishes these things of her bag: 1.) Stinkfoot's kneepants & propeller beanie, 2.) Moll's old muzzle, and 3.) their telling baby pictures. We know all this because Mrs B. proudly holds them up & mouths their owner's names.

STINKFOOT *(as himself)* - How ya doin', Ma?
(imitating Mrs Bag Bag) - Okay, son. Are you still going through college?
(as himself) - No, ma. I'm a dentist now, with my own expanding practice.
(imitating Mrs Bag Bag) - Oh, son, I should be so proud - but you know your father...
(as himself) - Frankly, no, I don't ma.
(imitating Mrs Bag Bag) - And Moll, did she ever become a nurse?
(as himself) - Heck, I don't know, ma. I don't give a poop. I ain't seen her in nine years.
(to the audience, referring to Mrs Bag Bag) See what I mean? Even though all it took was a tin of salmon to steal my heart - she loves me. *(to Polly, & suddenly)* Pollyanna! You ever hear that name? Parakeet to Meetcha? No? But the way you look? It's funny - I can't seem to put my finger on it.

Isaiah *(crowding Polly)* - An' you're not going to!

Stinkfoot looks at Mrs Bag Bag, at Elma, who's been making a bed out of more bags, then luxuriantly lying on them, at Polly, who has hung on his every word making fluttery flying movements now and again, even at Isaiah, the disgruntled flatfish.

STINKFOOT - Funny thing... I never thought I'd say it, but - hey! It's good to be home. Sort of.

Comes the beat of (offstage) jungle drums, and a sudden ARRRGGGGHHHH! The Partly Cooked Shrimp rushes on.

PARTLY COOKED SHRIMP *(listens for drums, gone suddenly silent)* - By the whelks, they've stopped!

And up comes THE MEOW BLUES. Whereupon Stinkfoot yowls:

THE MEOW BLUES

Out there, it's a jungle. Down here it's a jungle.
Up there in Soliquisto's Ivory Tower jungle...
At the top of the world, the end of the pier jungle -
There ain't no culture. There ain't no law. There ain't no rules.
'Cept one - you gotta fight!
You gotta keep on hooowwwlin! You gotta
keep on sayin': This is me and I'm alive! I'm alive-ooh!
(to all on the beach)
Now come on, say it to me. This is me -
ALL - This is me!
STINKFOOT - And I'm alive!
ALL - And I'm alive!
STINKFOOT - And I'm hungry an' I got red blood in me!
And my red blood loves those scary teeth -
Let me bite cha!
Oh, I got growlin' love. Howlin' love!
I got the... got the... Meow Blues!
CHORUS - Yowl! Rowl! Growl! Snarl! etc.

The lids of the three barnacles pop open & shut, syncopated, and off-stage, from somewhere on the pier above them, Moll's voice joins in. Elma does one hell of a jazzy electric St. Elmo's Dancing Jig with the Partly Cooked Shrimp. Mrs Bag Bag, after listening for a moment, shrugs & disappears back in her bag

MOLL *(offstage)* - Owwww!!! I can hear my old man howling,
  With his wishbone cough, he can never get enough.
  You…. can hear him yowlin' -
  He won't throw in the towel 'til he struts his stuff!
  Ohhhh…. it's the old old story - who's gonna score me tonight?
  Ohhh, I'm feelin horny!
  But you gotta understand: that's my old man!

  You gotta make your bed and there you lies…
  When the moon comes out - you advertise.
  When the red tomcat wants to sow his seed…
  Basically, well - yes, indeed.

Just as the song finishes, a light comes on in the window above them. In it Soliquisto sits quietly, his head cocked towards the beach below, listening.

SOLIQUISTO - The voices of the sea! But poor Soliquisto hears only the music of Stinkfoot! No, no - it's being back here… it's this, this… place that makes the sound of the sea sound like he. It is not yet madness - is it?

In a kind of a Pied Piper Bourbon Street Blues procession, all follow the dancing Stinkfoot off - all except the bagged Mrs Bag Bag who is now merely a humming lump on the stage.

Lights fade to Black.

ENTR'ACTE.

LUNCHTIME COFFEE HOUSE

& COMEDYTHEATRE & MUSIC HU
& ROCK & ROLL & JUMP & JAZZ &
& ART & DARTS & 1985 & IM PROI
& LATE.LATE BAR & Bistro EA

ACT TWO, SCENE ONE.

Still under the pier - some indefinite time later. Up in the lit window, Moll & Buster (on ukulele) work out a new song... more of:

THE MEOW BLUES

MOLL *(speaks)* - I get it, Buster. Yowl, scowl, howl, growl!
(sings) You need a hot tin roof to sing the Meow Blues,
You need a dirty backyard in the city stews -
You need a washing line where the washings not.
Basically that's all you got.
You need a red tomcat with juju eyes,
With his ear torn off in an alley fight.
When the red tomcat comes up to scratch -
Basically, stay offa my patch.
(Buster joins in) Yowl! Scowl, howl, growl!

Slowly being lit as the window above goes dark, Stinkfoot is sitting with his back to the audience, leaning on a barnacle. He's looking out to sea as he listens to the offstage row coming from the dressing room over his head.

SOLIQUISTO *(offstage) (angry)* - I am sorry, Buster. I cannot allow it on my stage.

BUSTER *(offstage)* - You might at least let me try, Uncle. Audiences like a bit... of... music.

Stinkfoot holds up a speech balloon: BACK IN THE OLD ROUTINE. HA.

SOLIQUISTO *(offstage)* - Do not presume to tell me about audiences.

Louder than these two, Moll hisses & laughs. Alarmed, Stinkfoot looks up, down, sideways. Gives out a small hiss himself.

BUSTER *(offstage)* - But Uncle...
SOLIQUISTO *(offstage)* - Be quiet. I am thinking!
SCREWY *(offstage)* - Well, that's what he calls it.
BUSTER *(offstage)* - That's all you ever do - I do all the bloody work. Listen to this - *(plunk-plunk-plunking sound of a ukulele)*
SOLIQUISTO *(offstage)* - Dammit!

There is the noise of a scuffle and the uke flies through the window, only to land in Stinkfoot's causally outstretched paw. With gusto, he begins to strum. Then jumps up to dance & sing.

LANDING ON MY FEET FEET

Throw me out your window... sling me in the street,
Drop me from a high, high height - I land on my feet feet.
Brush me down and dust me, I won't even slow down.
Suckers, you c'n trust me - trust me just to go, go, go!
In any situation, I can turn a trick.
It's no hallucination... I land on my feet feet, yes I do.
Lookin' for an angle - lookin' for a blow-ow-ow!
Stick me in spot light - Watch me do a show-ow-ow!
Landin' on my feet feet, landin' on my feet - yeah!
Try to knock me over - I land on my feet.

And as he winds down, Polly enters. With little hops & skips and half flaps, she does not notice him until circling her, he yells:

STINKFOOT - Hey, Budgie. Don't begrudge me! *(Polly awks in surprise)* A-rootie, hang on cutie. Tonight's the night for your solo flight. All right!

POLLY - That's what Mrs Bag Bag says, well... not like you say it, of course. She says, *(imitates Mrs B.)* The bags tell me, the bags say, time to be up - & away. *(the usual Polly)* But how did you know?

STINKFOOT - Hey, she's my own ma, ain't she? It's in the blood, kiddo. So I know you tryin' to fly. And I know that's natural. But where you goin'? That could take some 'splainin'. *(to audience)* An' it could be entertainin'. *(to Polly)* You want to go up - then what's a sweet kid like you doin' down?

POLLY *(with another little awkward hop & flap)* - You wouldn't understand. You're never down.

STINKFOOT - True.

POLLY - And you can do anything.

STINKFOOT - That's true too. But it's easy. You just gotta wanna. Lookit. *(he cartwheels, duck walks, whatever - it's all smooth & effortless)*

Polly watches all this astounded. She lifts a wing, looks at it, drops it. Looks at her big bird feet, tries to tap, stops it. Feels her feathery bum - could she lay an egg? Mimes that. Mimes breaking it.

STINKFOOT - Anything I can do, you can do - almost. All I ever did was watch and listen... I learned by listening to the old man up there. *(he points upwards)*

POLLY *(cleaning egg off her hands)* - God taught you all that?

STINKFOOT *(gives her a look)* - Nah. Soliquisto. Ventriloquisto? *(mimes hand up his back)* Mephisto? *(makes horns of his fingers)* Psychologisto? *(mimes a strait jacket) (to audience)* Apologisto? Well eggy, peggy leggy, I should coco! *(to Polly)* Get the gist? Forgeddit! Let me teacher cos' I can reach yer. *(whistles)* You wanna whistle? Pucker up & toot. Go on, will ya. *(she tries, and can't)* Forgeddit. Listen. Learnin' how ain't hard. It's seizin' the moment, lettin' it foment. It's comin' through with a brew that's new. Woo-oo. Get it? Never, never, never, *never* despair. *(to audience)* This is Stinkfoot talkin' - and I learned it up there.

Enter Isaiah with a conch shell. Finding both Stinkfoot and Polly together, and both looking up, he too looks up. At what? Like a spyglass, he looks through his conch.

ISAIAH - There's a whole lotta mud up there, whole lotta mud. *(he blows through the conch & it wails)*
STINKFOOT - There's one conch who's out to lunch.

Enter a scuttling Mrs Bag Bag with Elma writhing just behind.

MRS BAG BAG - A bird is a peck. A cat is a scratch. You are a sorry sole. And that's mine.

So saying, Mrs Bag Bag snatches the conch shell away from Isaiah and stuffs it in her bag. Elma sways up to the edge of the stage and vamps the audience. Polly goes back to her hop-flapping. Stinkfoot loves everything everyone does.

ISAIAH *(to audience) (very mournful)* - Do you know why lobsters won't share their lunch?
STINKFOOT *(happily falling in with the corny old music hall routine)* No. Why won't lobsters share their lunch?
ISAIAH - Because they're shellfish. Ha. Ha.
STINKFOOT *(can't help himself; this is what he is)* - Say? You ever hear the one about the self-conscious conch?
POLLY *(out of patience, with herself & everyone else)* - Every single one of you... you're all, you're all - stuck in the mud. *(points at each one except Stinkfoot who is impishly encouraging All in their behaviour)* But not me, not me. I'm getting out of here.
ELMA *(her attention finally caught by something other than herself)* - Out of here? Where is 'out of here'? There is only the deep - and the deep is mine. You do not swim. You do not dive.
POLLY *(flaps like mad)* - But... I... will... fly.

Music building: IMAGINATION.

POLLY *(sings)* - Imagination is all I've ever called home.
  But imagination can leave you out in the cold.
  What I'm looking for is something real and it doesn't grow on trees
  But if I don't make it, will you respect me please?
MRS BAG BAG *(speaks)* - Not make it? Of course you will make it.
POLLY *(SINGS)* - Empty handed, I stand before the unknown,

Hear me breathing, whoever is out there - hello.
If I take this giant leap, catch me if you can...
Whoever is out there - understand.
MRS BAG BAG *(imitates her flapping attempts)* - Not to understand, dear - to fly! You just fly away home.

At the word 'home', Elma looks at the sea, Mrs Bag Bag looks in her bags, Isaiah looks at Polly, Stinkfoot looks up (musical quote: FOLLOW YOUR NOSE), and Polly bursts into tears, collapsing onto The Bags.

STINKFOOT *(now semi-serious)* - Hey, budgie - don't misjudge me. Listen! All this business of feelin' bad and feelin' down is bad for business - and the business is livin'. You leave it to the cannibals up there *(points with Buster's uke)* to feed off themselves.
POLLY *(snivelling)* - You're the worst of the lot. All you do is show off.
STINKFOOT - But that's Stinkfoot, kiddo. That's me. What you gotta do is help yourself. Like the judge said to the judge - *(shoo-ing her back up again)* Try yourself, man. And then you be the judge. *(to audience)* Me oh my. Now we cookin'. I should coco. Yeah, now we're cookin'.
ISAIAH - And we're not the only ones. What's pink and nasty looking that shrinks in boiling water?

Enter Partly Cooked Shrimp, screaming. Exit Partly Cooked Shrimp, screaming.

ISAIAH - Oh dear. There's one prawn every minute. Am I right or am I wrong?
STINKFOOT *(completely convinced)* - Right!
POLLY - Rubbish!
MRS BAG BAG - Rubbish is as rubbish does. *(pulling a magic lantern out of her bag, she rubs it)* And here's the rub. *(comes a puff of intriguing smoke, though no one notices)*
Elma *(grabbing Stinkfoot by his lapels and 'tossing him away')* - Nothing is worth keeping - if you cannot throw it away.

Elma begins to pull things out of Mrs B.'s bags & scatter them. With a screech, Mrs Bag Bag gathers them up again. Isaiah furtively retrieves his conch.

POLLY - Everyone else is, they're all... well, they're...
STINKFOOT - Nuts?

POLLY *(to Mrs Bag Bag)* - And you! You never tell me anything I want to know.

MRS BAG BAG *(clutching her smoking lantern)* - What do you want to know, dear?

POLLY - Where did I come from?

MRS BAG BAG - From an egg, dear.

POLLY - But where did the egg come from?

All shush Isaiah before he can answer that one.

MRS BAG BAG - From up there, dear. And someday, if you wait...

ISAIAH - Oh dear, dear, dear, dear, dear...

POLLY - Oh, shut up! *(to Mrs Bag Bag)* - I am sick of waiting.

ISAIAH *(hands her his conch)* - Listen to this.

POLLY *(puts it to her ear, and listens, and listens, and listens)*
(finally) I can't hear anything.

ISAIAH - I know. It's been like that all morning. *(in an attempt to woo her)* I've got a weight problem. That's why I'm on a seafood diet. I...

STINKFOOT *(interrupting)* - Every time you see food, you eat it!

Polly turns her back on all of them, beginning to croon with music under: IMAGINATION. She flaps & she skips & she swoops & she jumps. And Stinkfoot, noticing this, follows, flapping & skipping & jumping. And then, one by one, they All notice, so, one by one, they follow, flapping & skipping & jumping. The smoke from Mrs B.'s lantern grows thicker.

STINKFOOT - G'wan, kiddo. You can do it. I believe in you. I believe! I always said so. Oh, my lordie!

On a jump, Polly rises, only to sink. Then rises again, higher - surprised, tentative.

MRS BAG BAG - What can you see, dear?

POLLY *(ecstatic)* - More!

Polly comes lightly back to earth... and the smoke grows thicker. But with one more jump, she is airborne and 'flying' just above their heads. All duck.

ISAIAH - I'm not worried - if she does fall, 'er body will cushion 'er from the shock.

IMAGINATION

Imagination, you knew I'd make it come true!
For a month of Sundays, I've been relying on you.
Where I dreamed I'd go, I can go... set sail on any breeze.
Imagination .. would you take me home now, please?

Imagination can lift you out of the cold.
Imagination will never ever grow old.
A magic carpet, it's fairy dust, it's all here in my mind.
Here's lookin at you - me? I'm gonna fly.

Joyful hearted, I sail into the unknown.
Hear me breathing... whoever is out there - hello.
I've just taken a giant leap -
Catch up to me if you can.
Whoever is out there - I understand...
All I become, I will be.
What I become - will be me!

Over the rainbow, further than elephants fly -
Polychrome's daughter, Sindbad the Sailor am I.
What I've been looking for I have found, right here in my dreams
Imagination is everything - it seems!

And then - she flies up and out of sight into the smoke.

STINKFOOT *(to audience)* - Now *there's* a show stopper. Say? Wonder if she needs a partner?

So saying, he scampers up a pier piling after her.
Fade to Blackout.

ACT TWO, SCENE TWO.

Lights up to an empty backstage. From offstage (which is, of course, 'on stage') comes hearty applause. Followed moments later by Buster wheeling Soliquisto into the dressing room. A very alert Screwy sits in Sol's lap. Buster goes back to perform (he is given a warm os welcome) while Soliquisto hops up to put Screwy in the wheelchair and pushes the chair forward until it is front & centre stage.

Screwy jumps out of the wheelchair, and - with a great flourish - offers it to Soliquisto. There follows a no! yes! no! oh, go ahead, you need it more than me 'dumb routine' until Solly gives up and sits in the chair. Immediately Screwy sits on his lap.

SOLIQUISTO *(lights a cigarette)* - We don't get much of a chance to be alone - I miss it.

SCREWY - Shouldn't you be drinking a glass of water while I'm talking? Lost the knack, have we?

Soliquisto throws back his head and gargle-argle-argles.

SCREWY *(over the gargling)* - We are most impressed. We don't say! *(puffs on Sol's offered cigarette, & coughs)*

SOLIQUISTO *(to his mirrored reflection)* - I smoke too much.

SCREWY - You're worried. Worry. Worry. Worry. Horrified, you are. It's understandable. Any bloke facing what you're facing... well, I hate to see any bloke crack up - Sir! Big feller like yourself, too. But I've seen it! Oh yes. Seen it in the trenches! Seen it in the confessional! Sir! Any bloke under fire is likely to crack! Sir!

SOLIQUISTO - I am not any bloke... I'm...

SCREWY - Crack!

SOLIQUISTO - I am...

SCREWY *(nasty & sharp)* - Crack! Well, oo' are you? Doctor Frankenstein?

SOLIQUISTO - Don't be silly.

SCREWY - Dr. Jekyll?

SOLIQUISTO - Stop it.

SCREWY - Caligari? Machiavelli? Svengali?

SOLIQUISTO - Stop it!

SCREWY - Stop it!

Enter Buster in his cat costume. On a snare drum, he practices a drum break - endlessly. Up comes SURE AS EGGS IS EGGS.

SCREWY - Arrest that man and force him to face himself. Eyes right!

SOLIQUISTO - Oh, for god's sake.

SCREWY - Force him to force himself, sergeant. *(to audience)* Is he wearing a falsehood? *(to Solly)* You'll never get a knighthood.

SOLIQUISTO *(weakly smiling)* - I'd never wear it.

Screwy jumps up for an exotic dance.

SCREWY - You don't deserve it.

SOLIQUISTO - I don't deserve *this*.

SCREWY - I don't care - me! Ha. Ha. I don't care! Do anything, lady! Yes! Bold as brass. Ha ha - me! Ha ha - you!

SOLIQUISTO - I don't know why I torture myself.

SCREWY - Don't ask me - I say what you say. What you say, I say. But it *is* nice to be alone - you said so! Sir! *(Soliquisto looks longingly at his dummy's box)* Put me back in the box - but that won't stop it. That won't stop me. I'll be with you - and you'll be alone. You'll just carry on! Giving yourself grief. And only yourself to blame. What a carry on!

Buster performs his drum routine before his uncle.

BUSTER - I've got a new idea... about a dancing pope... *(Screwy collapses on the floor)* who loses his memory and winds up in a circus!

SOLIQUISTO *(mouths to his reflection - meaning towards audience)* - I hate you.

BUSTER - Ah, you're rehearsing. That's good. I'm always rehearsing. *(sings)* In nomine patris...

Soliquisto slowly rises from his wheelchair, obviously meaning to shove his dummy in its box. Painfully, he inches close, but as soon as he touches it, Screwy sits up...

SCREWY - And oo's got their hand up your back - God?

Polly appears at the open window... and hovers. She is curious rather than shy, suspicious rather than eager. If any comment she makes, it's a whistle or a chirrup. Buster is oblivious, but so soon as Soliquisto sees her, he leaps into the wheelchair. Screwy does an exorcist's double take.

SOLIQUISTO - I really *must* be cracking up - that's Pollyanna. *(holds out his finger as if she could alight on it)* Polly? Polly?
SCREWY - I wonder if the little bugger sings - Sir? Maybe she'd like to hear me play the piano - Sir?
SOLIQUISTO *(ignoring Screwy, he is transformed with tender eagerness)* You poor little thing. Come in. Come in. I won't hurt you.

Buster has finally noticed Polly, and stands staring at her, his jaw on his neck. He's horrified. He's disbelieving. He doesn't know whether to run away, swat her out of the sky, or pull her in. Buster is one comic reaction after another.

SOLIQUISTO *(wheeling himself close; as Polly flutters in, he circles her)* - Oh, yes! You are a brilliant creature - or you will be. A little preening, a little encouragement, a little love...
SCREWY - And very little pay.

Polly has seen her mother's picture. Buster is edging his way out of the room.

SOLIQUISTO *(in a froth of excitement)* - Yes. Yes. You are so very like her. But it's impossible. And yet? Perhaps if we had some music?

Comes a roar of applause from the 'stage', an offstage MEOW! HISS! from Moll. Polly reacts in fear. But Buster stops in his tracks. He can't go that way - where, where?

SOLIQUISTO - Buster! Lift Screwy to the piano. And you, you will oblige with a rhythm accompaniment! *(on his feet rummaging in his trunk; he shakes* out sheet music) Here it is! After so many years. *(to Polly)* You really are the very image of a very special artiste. *(announces)* 'Prince Pollyanna, the Queen of Songbirds' *(puts music on piano as Buster hoists Screwy to the bench)* As sung by herself! To great success! Before the crowned heads of Europe and far off lands! A comedy show-tune, written & composed by myself - with no unpleasant or surprising sharps or flats except in the choruses which are, as you will discover, enormously singable. Indeed, a song, which like my dutiful assistant, Buster, is both eager to please and simplicity itself. *(Buster gives him a dark look, but Polly is swept up by the fun of it; Screwy plays the intro: PARAKEET TO MEET YOU)* Enjoy yourself. Let go. Go on. That's it! In cockatoo-two time! One, two - cockatoo. Sing! Sing!

As Polly begins to sing, Soliquisto slumps exhausted into his wheelchair.

PARAKEET TO MEET YOU

(accompanied by a Whistling Chorus of offstage All)

I'm parakeet to meet you.
And cocka-doodle-too!
Macaw'll me Pollyanna -
But you know what toucan do!

I'm kookaburra-boom-de-ay.
Mais tu es mari - bou.
So keep yer cockatoo yerself -
Hoopoe-pooh to you!

All - Bugger off! Bugger off!
Ha ha ha ha ha ha ha ha!
Bugger off! Bugger off!

Jungle Bridge!

Smack in the midst of this cawing, crowing, whistling, hooting, screeching mayhem (that Soliquisto conducts in tired ecstasy), Persian Moll slams in from the 'stage'.

MOLL - What the bloody hell is this bloody row! They heard it back'a the house! *(spots Polly)* Meee-ow!

She leaps for the bird, all claws extended, but quick as quick, Buster is between them. Screwy, gleefully grinning, bangs away on the piano, while Soliquisto refuses to subscribe to this new reality, so still whistles furiously.

BUSTER - I won't have it, Moll. Not again. No. I mean it. She just flew in. She's nothing to you.

Suddenly noticing the audience, Moll must behave herself... so she arches her back and turns away. Buster urges Polly into a 'disappearing box' which has a Dutch door.

MOLL - Nothing that won't keep. *(seats herself near Soliquisto)* Hiya, Uncle Solly. Wasn't I good tonight?
SOLIQUISTO *(smiling sadly)* - When are you ever bad? I just can't bring myself to punish you - it's only your nature.
MOLL *(admiring her long nails, her sleek belly)* - You said it. I'm just naturally, ummm... hungry.
SCREWY - I am not responsible, Herr Ober. I gave the orders - I never did carry them out.
SOLIQUISTO - And I am... just a little bit frightened of you.

Moll smirks, and begins to groom herself.

BUSTER *(earnestly)* - She bloody terrifies me. It's all I can do to remember *(looks at her, horrified; she looks back, & snarls)* that she's only an animal. *(nervous)* Well, ha, ha - a very highly trained & clever animal.
SOLIQUISTO *(smug)* - Well, yes... and I suppose I should take credit for her...
SCREWY - Lack of humanity, Sir?
SOLIQUISTO *(a little bit shocked, but carrying on)* - There must, of course, be a certain amount of cold-bloodedness - after all: The Show Must Go On! But a truly *human* being does have a responsibility...

Buster, no longer listening, checks the 'disappearing box' to make sure Polly is still there.

She isn't. Did he dream her? Hallucinate her? Another series of Buster's over-the-top reactions behind Soliquisto, Screwy & Moll.

SOLIQUISTO *(confiding in the audience)* - The finest showbusiness is made much like a pilgrimage. Integrity, courage. Moral codes, spiritual values...

Moll stands, stretches, & pads to front of centre stage - she will talk & sing over what is going on behind her.

SCREWY - The quickchange artiste and the apostate priest. The physician and the magician. The bishop and the actress?
MOLL *(also confiding in the audience)* - One thing's for certain, and one thing's for sure - if my ol' man, Stinkfoot, ever came through that door, Uncle Sol would hafta cut the crap. When he saw Stinkfoot go zap, zap, zap!

Lights down to a follow spot on Moll as she sings:

SEE ME SOMETIME

Down there where you are, so humble & pure
So holy, unblemished and fine!
Well - I've had to claw and I've had to whore...
And I've had to fight for what's mine!
If you're one of the sheep, I'll make your flesh creep
With a whole catalogue of my crimes.
You may be shocked at the strokes I've concocted -
But I call it, stayin' alive! Yeow!
Come up & see me sometime.
You can come up and see me sometime -
If you dare.

During bluesy bridge, a second pin spot on Solly, obviously gone gaga... he steps into Screwy's box and is playing with a jack-in-the box. Up & down with Jack. Up & down. Screwy steps into the spot to stop him. Shakes its wooden head. No. No. No. Guides

Solly back to his chair. Sol's spot fades, and back to Moll.

If you wanna know, all my peccadilloes -
All the bad little things that I've done.
If you'll take the risk, here's a real life burlesque
'Bout a mean momma minx who loves fun, fun.

I got obsessed with bein' the best,
If you're not impressed, wait & see.
I've got the right to be myself tonight -
I'm a meteorite - burn with me! Yeow!

Come up & see me sometime.
You can come up and see me sometime.
If you dare.

Lights up at song's conclusion. Moll glides towards Soliquisto, taking a clawed swipe at his head as she passes behind him. Reflexively, he ducks. (Buster has disappeared during her song.)

SOLIQUISTO *(obviously babbling like this all along)* - Compassion, generosity. The courage to change! Live and let live! *(a humble laugh)* Oh, it's not easy... But those are the milestones, the indices of artistic growth.

SCREWY - It's been a pleasure serving under you, Sir. Especially now... when we're goin' *over the top* - together. Sir!

Moll hisses in disgust and withdraws behind her screen. But not before spotting a feather on the floor, picking it up, and tucking it down her cleavage.

SOLIQUISTO - Sometimes the way is hard, but often the burden is lightened with sweet, uplifting applause.

SCREWY - So give yourself a pat on the back, Sir!

SOLIQUISTO *(rising gracefully from his wheelchair)* - And always the way is unpredictable... you never know!

SCREWY - Just follow your nose up the yellow brick road, eh? Sir!

SOLIQUISTO *(transported)* - But what need we of compasses and maps,

When the spirit senses the wind - and knows the contours of all that breathes, And loves life's awful, cruel, uniqueness!

SCREWY - Why, all of a sudden a bloomin' great piece of cold wet haddock could smack you right on the back of the neck, Sir! Would pull you up with a bit of a nasty shock, Sir. Wouldn't it, Sir?

Soliquisto turns with real menace towards the dummy, just as Buster bustles back on stage dragging what looks like a raggedy doll along with him. In truth, it's Elma draped in kelp, 'playing dead' for safety.

BUSTER *(very excited)* - Look what I found! Me. I went out for a slash on the beach and there it was - right out in the open! Right there for the taking. Look what I can do with it!

Screwy, saved just in time, plays SPHINX & MINX, as Buster works with his 'doll' in a truly eccentric, very artful, bendy-doll dance.

For once, Soliquisto is impressed, actually pleased. His face is alight with the joy of something well done. And Buster, seeing his chance, drops the limp Elma, & rushes him. (Seeing her chance as well, Elma, the Electrifying Elver, slithers out the window. Small splash.)

BUSTER - We'll put it in the act. It'll go right after that magic thing you do...

SOLIQUISTO *(caught off guard)* - Well, no... you... it needs work.

BUSTER - Needs work? I saw your face - you liked it.

SOLIQUISTO - Well, yes... but it never hurts to make something perfect.

BUSTER *(for once, sensing he holds the high ground)* - Perfect? You taught me nothing's perfect - certainly not art. Each & ev'ry performance is only the best you can do. *For the moment.* So why this time, Uncle - why are you holding me back this time? *(looks around him, at the shabby room, at the maniacal Screwy)* You know what I think? I really don't think you know what the public wants - not anymore.

SOLIQUISTO *(grown rigidly furious)* - What the public wants? What my public wants? I know what my public wants from me!

Soliquisto towers in red melodramatic majesty to sing:

WHAT MY PUBLIC WANTS

I know what my public wants...
What my public wants is blood!
They don't give a toss for art or fart -
They wants to see you bleed!

If an artist you would be -
First admit defeat.
Don't bother with the fruit & veg -
But go heavy on the meat!

Screwy, Buster & Offstage Chorus:

He knows what his public wants...
What his public wants is blood.
They don't give a toss for niceties -
They wanna see you bleed.
Cos': they wants yer, they wants yer,
They wants yer, they wants yer, they wants yer,
They wants yer - they wants to see yer bleed!

Screwy (held up by Buster):

They'll mutilate and maim you
All in the name of fun.
The coroner's no foreigner -
He's an old friend like yer mum!

All & Chorus:

Da, da, da, da, da!
(whispering) They wants yer, etc.

Persian Moll (who has sashayed her way down front):

The public are too rude to think.

It's as much as they can do to get drunk.
But if your armour, they spot a chink -
They'll gouge out a chunk!

Chorus:

Da, da, da, da, da!
(whispered) They wants yer, etc.

Polly, obviously confused to find herself coming out of a hidden panel, reappears - wearing her mother's gorgeous stage clothes. (A big wonderful feathery creation.) Moll, spotting her, hisses & prepares to spring. But Buster, feeling confident ever since his dance with Elma, once more puts himself between them.

BUSTER *(firmly)* - No more blood, Moll. No more blood. Uncle, are you going to stop her - or am I? *(Soliquisto takes no notice, so Buster, like a lion tamer, cracks a whip)* Okay. Moll! Get back to you place! Back! Back!

Snarling, Moll slinks back to her place. Polly spreads her new & beautiful wings - and flies up to perch on something out of Moll's reach.

SCREWY - Somebody's trying to hurt me, Sir!
SOLIQUISTO - Stop it. Don't call me sir.

Meanwhile, the Chorus has continued - & does continue - whispering 'They wants yer'.

SCREWY - You're the only ranking officer left, Sir! The show must go on, Sir!
BUSTER *(shaking Screwy)* - You can't talk on your own!
SCREWY - Yes, I can. I know the secret.
BUSTER - Uncle! Uncle! Is this the only way I can get through to you?
SCREWY - Change and grow. Get rid of dead wood.
BUSTER *(aghast)* - What are you making me do?
SOLIQUISTO *(as his dummy)* - The show must go on, Sir!

Buster drags the dummy to the window - and throws it out. No splash, but a horrid thud. Polly flies gracefully down to centre stage - forcing Moll to one side.

POLLY *(sings)* - See the gorgeous ingenue -
A pretty girl and soon,
See the painted hag that she becomes
Whistling for the moon.

Enter The Public, covered in faces as the Chorus whispers: 'They wants yer, they wants yer, they wants yer....'

SOLIQUISTO *(bitterly sings)* - Give 'em all the gestures of Commedia dell
Arte.
BUSTER - Uncle!
SOLIQUISTO *(sings)* - But do be sure to give 'em gore...
BUSTER - Uncle!
SOLIQUISTO *(sings)* - If you want to join the party.
BUSTER - Uncle!
SOLIQUISTO - Do you mind?
BUSTER - Cut it out - Uncle, please.
SOLIQUISTO - If I have a cutting word, I sharpen it to blade. Ha ha ha!
BUSTER - Do you mind not talking when I'm talking!
SOLIQUISTO & BUSTER - I'm not talking when you're talking - you're talking
when I'm talking. I saw your lips move.

They both laugh - together for once. And here - Stinkfoot leaps through the window with Buster's ukulele.

STINKFOOT *(Cagney-brusque & bright)* - Hey, you guys - that's swell stuff. Real
old-timey, y'know. Nothin' like that in New York these days. Nah!
Gimme some Vaudeville, huh? Gimme some of dat ol' routine! *(taps &
pirouettes)*
BUSTER *(his first smile of sycophant greeting, now a rictus of astonishment)* - The old
routine! My god, it's you!
STINKFOOT - Yeah! It's all me. But don't bother with the starstuff, kiddo.
I'm real basic, right? Just treat me like one of the family. *(sticks out his
paw to Buster)* Put 'er there!

At the sight of Stinkfoot, Soliquisto seems to have gone halfway into catatonia. But Moll, without conscience, is delighted. Purring, she rubs herself against him.

STINKFOOT *(eyes her askance)* - Hey! Careful with the carcass, kittycat. You got fleas?

MOLL - I got catnip. I got cream. I got time… for mee-an-u-oow!

STINKFOOT - Hold that thought. Now, where was I?

BUSTER - You drowned.

STINKFOOT *(Brando-esque)* - You sleep with the fishes! *(over-acts choking)* It's an old Sicilian saying, Capiche?

BUSTER *(pointing at Moll)* - Forgive me. She… she… *(then)* Oh, bugger it. You're only a cat.

SOLIQUISTO *(semi-sanely)* - Is poor Screwy safely packed away?

STINKFOOT - Yeah. In a nice wooden suit. Me? I'm all broke up about it.

MOLL - But him… he's all broke up.

SOLIQUISTO *(brokenly)* - I never hurt anyone. Not really. I couldn't do that.

BUSTER *(to Moll & Stinkfoot who are grinning & circling each other)* - Stop it. Stop it! *(to Soliquisto) (kindly)* They're only animals. Trained animals. You trained them. But they don't have human feelings. You forgot that. You forget it now. *(quite sincerely)* Uncle Solly, you were once a completely wonderful man. But you don't practice what you preach. When Stinkfoot vanished - you should have let him go. Change & grow. Change & grow. All that stuff about the secret - I've forgotten it! Look - I've got a great new idea. It's about an artist. A serious artist.

SOLIQUISTO *(at the word 'artist', he shakes free of his torpor) (sings)* - If an artist you would be - first admit defeat! *(spoken)* I don't know why I torture myself. Put me back in me box!

BUSTER *(imitates Screwy)* - Then you'd be on yer own, Sir. If *you* say so!

SOLIQUISTO *(in mourning)* - Soliquisto contra mundus.

BUSTER - You are not alone. I'm with you. And…

STINKFOOT *(Mickey Roonily)* - Ah, c'mon Pop. G'wan - break a leg!

SOLIQUISTO *(rises to sing, smiling - giving out that old razzmatazz)* - Break your leg or break your mind…

MOLL *(sings)* - What the public wants is red!

SOLIQUISTO *(stronger)* - Break your heart or break your mind…

ALL TOGETHER INCLUDING CHORUS - They wants to see you bleed!

SOLIQUISTO *(singing sadly)* - If you reveal humanity…

MOLL *(sings)* - They'll knee you in the crotch!

SOLIQUISTO *(sings)* - At least in death there's dignity - so you might as well…

STINKFOOT *(sings)* - Bust a gut!

ALL PLUS CHORUS - Da da da da! They wants yer, etc.

As all sing, there comes a CLAP OF THUNDER, and Stinkfoot - who has slowly moved closer to the window - leaps out in a FLASH OF LIGHTNING.

MOLL (turning in time to see him go) (dismayed) - Oh, shit.

All freeze in astonishment.

Dead Blackout

(but under, and continuing, comes the whispered chorus:
'They wants yer, they wants yer, they wants yer...')

ACT TWO, SCENE THREE.

Lights up to find poor cast-off Screwy slumped on the beach. Headless, the dummy plays an accordion all by itself. (There's an occasional grumbling rumble now & then, with flashes of lightning out to sea.)

By and by, Stinkfoot comes walking along (like he does when he's alone, making faces & laughing), to stand and look down at Screwy with a kind of cocky sorrow. After all, head or no head, the dummy - in its way - is a fellow artiste. (Screwy's head is nearby, stuck in the sand.)

Stinkfoot sings:

IT'S WONDERFUL WHAT PEOPLE WILL DO

First you winds 'em up, and then ya lets 'em go.
It's wonderful what people will do.
First you makes 'em cross, and then ya makes 'em smile.
It's wonderful what people will do.
Human insecurity? Oh, what an opportunity!
It's wonderful what people will do.
A little pride? A little greed?
Me? I sow the mischief seed!

It's wonderful what people will do,
It's wonderful what people will do.

STINKFOOT *(leaning down to yell in Screwy's ear)* - 'allo? 'allo? 'allo!

From above & offstage, comes these calls:

SOLIQUISTO *(offstage)* - Stinkfoot, Stinkfoot, puss, puss, puss - come home!
MOLL *(offstage)* - Oooweee, Stinkfoot - have I got the hots for you!
BUSTER *(offstage)* - Uncle! Uncle! Uncle!
STINKFOOT *(listens with delight)* - Meee-ow! *(to Screwy)* Blimey, gov'nor - you've lorst your 'ead! Over a woman, was it? Over a woman? *(makes the dummy's head shake no, no)* Not over a woman - well! Must have been the wife. *(fixes the head back on the dummy's body, then jumps up to face the audience for one of his 'old routines')* I knew this bloke had trouble with his head. *(mimes hard of hearing)* Eh? Eh? Eh? What's the matter with ya?
SCREWY *(behind him, sits up straight)* - Eh? Eh? Eh? What's the matter with ya?
STINKFOOT *(jumps in surprise, but pleased to have a 'straight man')* - Well, anyway - he was a golfer, this bloke, and one afternoon he got a cricket ball... *(offstage THACK!)* stuck in his ear. Could not get it out for love or money. So he went to the doctor. Funny people, doctors. You never know where they've been. Anyway, the doctor said: 'allo? allo? yes, lady? Well, what do you expect? We all talk silly sometimes. *(offstage cacophony of Stinkfoot! Uncle! Puss! Puss! Puss!)* It's funny, isn't it?
SCREWY - You've got to laugh.
STINKFOOT - Anyway, now where was I? My father, whenever he blew off, used to stick his hand in front of his bottom. You don't see manners like that nowadays, do you? It's all vanished. Anyway, this bloke says to the doctor... I've got a cricket ball... *(offstage THWACK!)* stuck in me ear and all my friends are takin' the mick - help me, please. Funnily enough, the doctor was a bit deaf himself. He said: What's that? The bloke said, don't you start! *(crouching down by Screwy)* But there I was in the surgery... And this bloke comes up to me and ee' says...
SCREWY *(dropping its head on Stinkfoot's shoulder)* - Do you mind if I lean against you?
STINKFOOT - Whatever for? Are you feelin' faint?
SCREWY - I've gotta 'orrible skin disease... *(Stinkfoot leaps away & the dummy*

falls over) And the walls are a bit damp for it.

STINKFOOT - Well, we all talk funny sometimes. *(Again the offstage cacophony of Stinkfoot! Uncle! Puss! Puss! Puss!) (to Screwy when it doesn't speak its line)* Here, what's the matter, son? Cat got your tongue? I say, cat got your tongue?

Screwy, like a maniac jack-in-the-box, pops up to play its horrid accordion & sing:

WHY ME LEGS WON'T WORK

All me papers signed up, all me muscles lined up -
But oh, me brain's gone numb.
No perception, no direction -
I can't get offa my bum.
(Stinkfoot heaves it to its feet)
Wakkah wakkah wakkah wakkah way!
(Stinkfoot kicks one of its legs forward)
Wakkah wakkah wakkah wakkah way!
(Stinkfoot kicks the other leg forward)
Wakkah wakkah wakkah wakkah way!
*(Once again, Stinkfoot kicks the dummy... waits expectantly -
but silence, then, suddenly, as Stinkfoot would speak...)*
No instructions, oh, the ructions!
I might just go berserk.
No conception, no erection...
That's why me legs won't work.

STINKFOOT *(after a pause)* - Now, where was I?
SCREWY - You've got two brains inside your head.
STINKFOOT *(surprised, but fast on the uptake)* - Me? I'm lucky if I get the use of one. But yes, that's it! The brain. The doctor said: there's the left brain and then there's the right brain. I said, no wonder I'm in two minds all the time. But I always get me own way in the end. Laugh? Laugh? By the time I got off at the sixth floor it was running down me

legs like the juice out of a rhubarb tart. And may I remind you - this is a public lift! *(to someone in the audience)* You ever talk to yourself, lady? Well you can't help it, can you? It's a job to get anyone else to listen. *(stands behind Screwy and holds its stiff 'wooden' head) (sonorously)* Let's imagine ourselves inside Soliquisto's brain. *(looks up towards window)* Well, both his brains. Dark, isn't it? Poor old bloke. Tries so hard - and no one's going to thank him for it in the end.

Lights down on stage, to come up in the window above their heads. In it are strange faces, eerily lit. Two faces for the right side of the brain and two faces for the left. The Brain sings:

MURDER LIVING NEXT DOOR

BRAIN - We are indivisible, totally ourselves -
Connected by a corpus callosum.
RIGHT SIDE - But I call that a butterfly.
LEFT SIDE - And I call you a bore.
BRAIN - Oh, it's murder living next door.
RIGHT SIDE - I've just been in deepest bliss!
LEFT SIDE - What's the use of that?
BRAIN - Mostly we do not agree at all.
Listen to the neighbours, listen to the neighbours!
Oh, it's murder living next - oh, it's murder living next door.

Down below on the beach, Isaiah strolls on stage in his own spot, continuing the above.

ISAIAH *(sings)* - The only thing that worries me is doin' it alone.
Although I been doin' it a lot! With no one to encourage me,
I might become browned off...
I knew the answer once - but I forgot.
(speaks) Trouble is - I don't remember the bloomin' question either.
Turbot - or not turbot? Is that the question? Weather - will turn nasty?
No. Scrod or smelt?

As he stands there, perplexed by these weighty questions, the stage becomes bright with lightning & the gathering sounds of the storm. (Low, but building, music: THE ANGRY SEA) Quickly, he opens Polly's abandoned umbrella.

By lightning, we see Mrs Bag Bag amidst a bed of baby oysters, tenderly closing each one before the storm hits. But Elma is, as usual, asleep, tangled up in seaweed.

Stinkfoot, who naturally hates water, comes bounding on - pulling Screwy (with accordion) in an old, wheeled, deck-chair.

STINKFOOT (hops about, dodging raindrops) - Say, I thought New York had weather, but over here... (gets hit by a big cold drop down the back of the neck) Yeow! It's murder. It's... it's personal. Know what I mean? And speaking of murder...

Tremendous clap of thunder, which awakens Elma.

ELMA - Murder? (yawns) I like a good murder. It helps me to sleep.
STINKFOOT - Then this should knock you out. (points up) Any minute now, up there - someone's gonna get his.
SCREWY - Or hers. In which case, it would be murder most fowl.
STINKFOOT (he likes that) - Yeah! Like somebody's a dead duck.
ELMA - I can't tell if I am interested. Am I interested? (notices Screwy) That's interesting. I wonder if it likes fish? (she's off to vamp the dummy)
MRS BAG BAG (understanding immediately) - Then what are you doing down here, you contemptible cat? Polly is in danger.
ISAIAH - Polly? In danger?
STINKFOOT - Well now, let me see. Polly's a birdie. And Moll is like me - a cute little pussycat. What do you think?

As the sea & the music builds behind them, Isaiah looks at Mrs Bag Bag and she looks at him. This time, he has to do something. But what? Isaiah begins running in circles. But Mrs Bag Bag grabs something out of one of her bags, and thwacks Stinkfoot with it.

MRS BAG BAG - Do something audacious! Be spunky! Save her!
STINKFOOT - Gee, ma. That hurts. But okay, okay - jeeez, what a fella won't do for his old mum.

Comes the loudest thunderclap of all, and the stage plunges into darkness, the lights to come up again on a great wave sweeping out of the sea & up on the beach - to *carry them all away in a boiling roiling dance of waves & All.*

THE ANGRY SEA

A loud musical exchange between the orchestra, the sea & All. Adlibs, mayhem, & noise. Once again, the stage plunges into darkness.

Blackout

ACT TWO,
SCENE FOUR.

The backstage dressing room, where out the open windows the storm rages. Waves rise higher & higher. Soliquisto, Buster, & Polly are obviously 'on-stage' by the sound of it (music under THE ANGRY SEA is PARAKEET TO MEET YOU). Amidst the usual, sits something new: a rather large bird's cage.

Suddenly, right through the windows, comes a tumbling, rolling, flailing Stinkfoot, Screwy (plus accordion), Mrs Bag Bag, and Elma, the Electrifying Elver.

ISAIAH *(out at sea, heard but not seen)* - Where's everybody gone? I can't see a bloomin' thing! Not with these eyes!

The only one who hasn't been here before is Mrs Bag Bag. Wringing out a bag she has managed to bring along, she immediately begins snooping.

ELMA *(just before hiding in the travelling trunk)* - I am not dead. I do not dream. Do I like this place?

But Stinkfoot hops right up, shakes all four of his paws, and props Screwy on the piano bench (who immediately plays a little: SONG OF THE SAW).

STINKFOOT *(paw cupped to ear)* - Well, ma... here we are. And by the sound of things, the goose ain't been cooked yet.
SCREWY - Shred, shred, the tweety bird's dead... But what's incisors for!
MRS BAG BAG - Stinkfoot! You stop that!
STINKFOOT - It ain't me, ma. It's *him*.

On the word 'him', Soliquisto enters. It's Solly that Stinkfoot obviously means.

SOLIQUISTO - Stinkfoot! You've come back! And, my word, there's Screwy too...

SCREWY - Can't keep a hard man down - Sir!

SOLIQUISTO *(spots Mrs Bag Bag) (a bit unnerved)* - And this is... this is - oh my god. Is that her!

STINKFOOT - This is ma. And ma, this is the man upstairs.

MRS BAG BAG *(nose to nose with Solly)* - What have you done to Polly, you great lump?

SOLIQUISTO - She went out there an ingenue - but she'll come back a star!

Much offstage applause & in comes Polly in another of her mother's gorgeous costumes. She is flushed and triumphant. She rushes to Mrs B.

POLLY - Oh, Mrs Bag Bag... I know who I am!

MRS BAG BAG *(popping Solly's jack-in-the-box in her bag, she eyes the cage)* - You are who you are - it's what you are that counts. But that's nice, dear.

With a proprietary air, Soliquisto steers Polly away from the mad bag lady and towards her cage. Polly hops right in & settles there, the picture of contentment. Mrs Bag Bag looks at it, looks at her bag, realizes it won't fit - and shrugs. Off to find smaller pickings.

SOLIQUISTO *(holding out his arms to embrace his 'creations')* - Well! Now that Stinkfoot's come home...

STINKFOOT - I been meaning to talk to you about that, Sol... I been...

SOLIQUISTO *(oblivious of all else)* - ... I'm sure Moll will be herself once more. And with our new singing Songbird! Why! The sky is, Once more... the limit. We...

Enter Buster, who undergoes his usual conflicted reactions to finding the dressing room full of threat & promise.

SOLIQUISTO - ... will play theatres again, proper theatres. There will be marquees & lights & perhaps...even - a command performance! Buster!

BUSTER *(getting very excited)* - Uncle?

SOLIQUISTO - Call my agent. Pack our trunks. *(Buster begins trying to do everything at once)* No. No! First we will create a new routine. Something serious... wait! Didn't you say you'd already written one... about a serious artist?

BUSTER *(can't believe his ears)* - Yes. Yes! It's right here in the trunk. *(opening the trunk to find his new routine, he finds instead... Elma)* Hey! Look at this, here's my dancing doll. I wondered where I put it... *(as he hauls her out, Elma is alarmed, but limp)*

STINKFOOT - Say that's... that's... *(Mrs B. kicks him)* That's nice.

SOLIQUISTO - Screwy! Play something for Buster to dance to. *(Screwy, reflecting Solly's joy, begins WHAT MY PUBLIC WANTS)* No. Not that - something lyrical, something 'serious'.

Screwy begins IMAGINATION. And Buster begins a beautiful waltz with Elma. As they dance, Elma sparks and fizzes; she comes alive to 'performing'.

SOLIQUISTO *(so pleased)* - Yes, that's what we want. A moment of grace.

SCREWY - There won't be a dry seat in the house, Sir.

Enter, unobserved, Moll, who stops (extreme stage right) at the sight of the dancing eel.

MOLL *(to audience in a huge 'stage whisper')* - Fish!

Buster brings the dance to conclusion, but Elma would go on - and on.

STINKFOOT *(who's been trying to say this all along)* - Listen, Solly, here's what I'm thinkin'. Me & Polly here... *(Polly, who's been preening her new feathers, perks up)* we're going to New York. I gotta offer for a Broadway show I can't refuse. And with Polly as a partner, I can count the movie deals already... *(to Polly)* You comin' with me, kiddo? You wanna play Broadway? You wanna see your name up in lights on the Great White Way?

POLLY *(very simple, charmingly humble)* - Yes.

SCREWY - You'll need a piano player - Sir! I come cheap.

SOLIQUISTO *(truly devastated by this turns of events)* - Oh, Screwy - you too betray me in my hour of weakness?

SCREWY - Ready when you are. Sir!

Buster drops Elma (who dives out the window) to tend to his stricken uncle. Solly has fallen back into his wheelchair, hand over his broken heart. Mrs Bag Bag is looking at Screwy. At her bag, at the dummy, at the window, at her bag. Will it fit? The dummy is

looking at Mrs Bag Bag. Is she screwy?
  But Moll, still on the sidelines, is galvanized. After all, the movies sound just up her alley.

MOLL - Stinkfoot! You know there's no better partner for you - than me.
STINKFOOT *(torn, but dubious)* - Well, it's not like you ain't got the talent, puss... an' it ain't like you can't be a great partner when you partner, pard. And it ain't like you're not my girl, but... *(looks at Buster, who looks away; at Screwy who looks from Mrs Bag Bag to Moll and back again. Danger on every side.)* But you're kinda *fatal*, you know?

Moll makes a bid for sympathy as she sings:

ONLY BEING MYSELF

I haven't felt anything like this in a long time -
I've been looking outside the wrong way for too long.
Blinded by my selfish need... and never letting go.
Now I need to let you know - oh, my friends -
Today I'm free.
Finding peace within myself, I never knew I could.
I had all the answers, but I misunderstood.
Taking love from others is simple, sometimes greed.
I know it's easier to take than to forgive.
I know now - it's easier to take than to forgive.
ALL - Who are you?
MOLL - But I'm begging you, please trust me again.
ALL - Who are you?
MOLL - I'd understand if you said: no, no, no!
But please, let me explain.
(to Stinkfoot who loves it - but doesn't buy it)
Please believe that all my crossin' over..
Only proved to me my love for you.
I was livin' only me, I was lovin' only me.
(behind her paw to audience) I only hope he buys this switcheroo.

Now I'm become myself... I can love you.
Only bein' myself.
I see the light for the first time in my life -
I'm begging you, don't make me beg.
There's no excuse in me, I feel new juice in me.
STINKFOOT - Oh, pull the other leg.

Throughout, Solly has listened intently - now as Moll mimes sincerity, he sings out - capturing the attention of all.

SOLIQUISTO - Who am I?
ALL - Who are you?
SOLIQUISTO - I'm begging you...
ALL - Who are you?
Whooooo?

Soliquisto stands up from his wheelchair, strides to the disappearing box, opens the door, and steps inside. The door slams with a great CRACK!
Buster jumps forward to open the box, and finds nothing.

Fade to Blackout

ACT TWO,
SCENE FIVE.

Music under: DAN, DAN. Calling voices sing: 'Soliquisto, Soliquisto' - over & over. (This entire scene is played over a woven medley of songs gone before.)

Lights slowly up on the seemingly deserted beach. No cocklesheds, no barnacles, no rockpools... just oddments of beach trash, a deserted deck-chair, and Soliquisto - who appears a broken man. The music fades for a moment so that we can hear the tumbling sound of the surf.

Solly walks towards the sea. Does he think of drowning himself?

(Music changes to DROWNED SAILOR'S DREAM) Comes the voice of Elma, and then, far out at sea, Elma herself swimming in & out of the waves.

ELMA - I sing to you as a diver arc-ing deep!
   I sing to you of a secret only you can keep.
   Be with me - sailor.
   Come to me - sailor. Here I am - sailor.

Elma dives and is gone.

(Music: 'Grumble Grumble Grumble' from YOU CAN'T CONFOUND A FLOUNDER)

Bewitched in spite of himself, Soliquisto has sat on what he thinks is a rock... but it's Isaiah, buried in the sand.

SOLIQUISTO *(jumping up)* - Good grief, I'm so sorry.

ISAIAH *(sitting up long enough to sing)* - Oh, dear... dear, dear... dear dear... dear dear.
   Life is just a muddle, so I live in a puddle,
   and all that I presume - is gloom.

(music: SPHINX & MINX) Enter Mrs Bag Bag pulling her largest bag which is obviously full of something heavy.

MRS BAG BAG - Does it make you feel uneasy,
  Thinking that I'm going crazy?
  What do I hide so deep inside
  Me bag, bag, bag, bag, bag, bag, bag?
  (sees Soliquisto) Here - you! Help me with this.

Even in extremis, ever the gentleman, Soliquisto hastens to assist her. (music: WHY ME LEGS WON'T WORK) With all their tugging, out tumbles Screwy and the accordion.

SCREWY *(head pops up, sees the audience, sees Solly looking screwier than he does)*
  - Have you gone soft, sir? There are ladies present. Get me up. Get me
  up. *(Solly complies, and Screwy plays the accordion)*
  (sings) All my keys are wound up, all me muscles bound up,
  I might just go berserk.
SOLIQUISTO - Tell me the truth, Screwy - am I all washed up? Is this the
  end of the Great Soliquisto?

Screwy stares at him. Soliquisto stares at Screwy. As they lock lunatic eyes, up comes the music of WHAT MY PUBLIC WANTS.

BUSTER *(offstage)* - Uncle? Where are you, uncle?

Whispered Chorus over: 'We wants yer, we wants yer, we wants yer...'. as Screwy falls over, and Soliquisto looks for a place to hide. Short of burying himself in the sand like Isaiah, there is no where to go.
  Enter a truly concerned Buster. Followed by a worried Polly, and the capering, unsinkable, duo of Stinkfoot and Moll.

BUSTER - I've looked everywhere for you - uncle, are you all right?

(music changing to: ONLY BEING MYSELF.)

SOLIQUISTO - I am alone and I am lost. I created them all. I created each
  & every one of them from the thin uncaring air. *(Mrs Bag Bag shakes her
  head, not me, not me - I am myself.)*
  (almost a whisper) I created myself. And now I am my own monster. I

am... I am...

MRS BAG BAG *(singing)* - Who are you?

SOLIQUISTO - I am...

ALL *(singing)* - Who are yooouuu?

SOLIQUISTO *(gestures towards Stinkfoot, Moll, and Polly)* - ...nothing, Not without my art. My creations.

BUSTER *(tenderly)* - No, uncle - you have you. Do the work and let it go. Let your creatures go! You are a great artist - and a great artist can always make more.

Behind them, Elma has wriggled out of the water, and now dances on the beach - she is a thing of unfettered beauty. Heedless of what goes on around her, she whirls by Buster and Solly.

SOLIQUISTO *(cannot help himself; he is entranced by Elma, he follows her every move)* - I can... always... make - more?

BUSTER - Haven't you always made more? Isn't there always more to make?

Soliquisto has actually heard Buster, really heard him. His finished work is let loose in the world: Stinkfoot and Polly and Moll will live or die without him - already they're dancing away up the beach with Mrs Bag Bag. But here, before him, young and fresh and unfinished, is new art, new work - 'more'.

SOLIQUISTO *(breaks into song)* - I see the light for the first time in my life...

BUSTER *(sings)* - I'm begging you, don't make me beg.

SOLIQUISTO *(sings)* - There's no excuse in me, I feel new juice in me.

STINKFOOT *(at a distance, singing)* - Oh, pull the other leg.

BUSTER - Come on, Uncle Solly. Let's go... let's carry on.

SCREWY - Oh, what a carry on!

(music becomes: NO TIME LIKE THE FUTURE)

Solly smiles at his faithful nephew, and so with a bow & a great Oscar Wildean flourish, gestures Westward ho!

SOLIQUISTO - Away with us. New worlds await our genius! *(turning back towards Elma)* You there!

ELMA - You speak to me?

SOLIQUISTO - I could make you a star.

ELMA - A starfish?
SOLIQUISTO - Exactly!

Buster gathers up the fallen Screwy and puts him in the deckchair. As he and Soliquisto walk away (no, skip away!), wheeling Screwy, all the rest (including Isaiah) return by methods various to front & centre stage, singing: you say there is no time, you say there is no time.
   Solly, Screwy and Buster exit.

ISAIAH *(sings)* - But now's the time, now's the time.
ALL - The moon follows - the old patterns, are
   taking place in the sky...
MRS BAG BAG - Here am I, filled with wonder.
POLLY - And I'm flyin'.
ALL - The sea follows the moon patterns,
   the waves whisper to tides. Change is the whole of your life...
ELMA - Keep on diving.
STINKFOOT - You say there is no time like the future. But now's the time...
ALL - Now's the time.
MOLL - But I'm still looking forward to what used to be...
ALL - But now's the time...
   Now's the time.

Just before
Blackout,
Stinkfoot gives out a great yowl and cartwheels across the stage.
Music out with the BUGGER OFF!
Chorus from PARAKEET TO MEET YOU that the whole cast sings in the dark.

OLD
PROFANITY

1985

BEAT THE BLACKMARKET BEASTS

CRACKPOT THEATRE PRESENTS:

STARRING:

Nikki B
as PERSIAN MOLL, A SIREN & THE LEFT HALF OF SCREWY'S BRAIN

John Beedell
as SCREWY, THE OCEAN LINER & CHORUS

Andy Black
as SOLIQUISTO & THE PARTLY COOKED SHRIMP

Pete Coggins
as ISAIAH, THE COASTGUARD & THE PUBLIC

Hirut
as ELMA & A WOEFUL SIREN

Steve Howe
as STINKFOOT, DROWNED SAILOR & THE BALANCED NOSE.

Tria Linning
as JELLYFISH, A WOEFUL SIREN & RAGGEDY ALMA

Sydney Longfellow
as MRS BAG BAG & A WOEFUL SIREN

Richard Smith
as BUSTER & THE GIANT SQUID

Cindy Stratton
as POLLY, A SIREN & THE RIGHT HALF OF SCREWY'S BRAIN

Desperate Men
& The Old Profanity Awkestra

The Old Profanity Showboat

The Grove, Floating Harbour   Bristol BS1 4RB   tel: 293301
EVENINGS - DECEMBER 7, 8, 9, 10, 11, 15 16, 17, 18, 19, 20, 21, 22, 23

Tickets now on sale

AT THE OLD PROFANITY SHOWBOAT & PARKS 51 RESTAURANT, PARK STREET, BRISTOL.
£5 for the evening performances, £3 for matinees

Light by **Paul Neville**
Choreography by **Vivian Stanshall** & **Tria Linning**
Music Director - **Pete Watson**
Costumes by **Caroline Poland**
Hair by **Nikki B** & **James** (Christian James Salon)
Set & Prop Painting by **Mark Millmore**
Stage Carpenter - **Mike Wilson**
Make-up by **Helen** & **Julie-Anna**
Mr and Mrs Stanshall's Girl Friday - **Julie Russell**
Stinkfoot Mascot & Sprite - **Silky Cyme Longfellow-Stanshall**

Special thanks to:

Stephen Fry, **Pete Moss**, **Mike Wilson**, **Julie Hawkins**, **Tim Streader**, **Tony Staveacre** & **Steve Poole** (BBC), **Jonathan Reekie**, **David Harrison** (Evening Post), **Richard Edwards** (HTV), **Peter Taylor** (Bristol Council), **Parks 51**, **Bob Redman**, **Bristol Old Vic Theatre School**, **Oasis PA**, **Sound Conceptions**, **The Toughs**, **Peter Ed**, **'Trilby'**, **Felicity Roma Bowers**, **Glen Armstrong** & **Fleur**

This edition was produced with the kind support of:
Fonds voor Beeldende Kunsten, Vormgeving en Bouwkunst,
Amsterdam

Stinkfoot & Old Profanity artwork:
Vivian Stanshall

Cover photograph of Vivian Stanshall:
Barrie Wentzell (www.galleryontheweb.com)

Cover photograph of Ki Longfellow-Stanshall:
Mush Emmons

The Stinkfoot photographs are from the collection of
Ki Longfellow-Stanshall and were taken by various people,
whose names have not been recorded or
whom we have been unable to trace

Design & Lay-out:
Ben Schot

Print:
De Nieuwe Grafische, Rotterdam

Special thanks to:
Sydney Longfellow

Sea Urchin Editions
PO Box 25212
3001 HE Rotterdam
The Netherlands
www.sea-urchin.net